Also From Florida Sportsman:

**Sport Fish of Florida
Baits, Rigs & Tackle
Fishing Planner
Best of Waterfront View**

**Florida Sportsman Magazine
Florida Sportsman Fishing Charts
Lawstick Law Guides**

From Hook to Table

By Vic Dunaway

Photographs by David Dunaway

Illustrations by Theodore R. Baker

WICKSTROM
PUBLISHERS, INCORPORATED
5901 S.W. 74 STREET, MIAMI, FLORIDA 33143

Answering the Big Questions...

For uncounted millions of recreational anglers, the catch of a potentially delectable fish immediately poses some big questions: What's the best way to clean the rascal? How can it be cooked? How should it be taken care of prior to cooking?

From Hook to Table answers those questions, and many more, handsomely and in depth.

The timing for this valuable new reference is perfect because there never has been so much interest in the healthful attributes of eating fish, which is an excellent protein source with little fat. And, of course, the many varieties of freshwater and saltwater fish offer an array of tantalizing possibilites for preparation, and their delicate shadings of flavor can only be brought out by careful attention to every step the angler takes between hook and table.

Proper care, preparation and recipe selection take on even more importance in the modern age of sports angling, when more and more fish are being released to fight again and the ones that are brought home to grace the sportsman's table are looked upon as special culinary treats deserving of the utmost attention.

Although he presents more than 100 recipes, author Vic Dunaway devotes no less attention to the important details involved in the basic methods of fish preparation—baking, broiling, sauteing, frying and poaching, along with barbecuing, smoking and campfire cooking. Just plain good eatin', if you will.

So land that fish and enjoy.

— *Karl Wickstrom*

Publisher

FOREWORD

Whether you catch all the fish that grace your table (or try to, anyway), or whether your fish dinners come from the local market, this book aims to make the handling, cleaning, cold-storing and cooking of your fish easier than it's ever been before. And the eating of them more delightful.

Here you'll find a guide to the table qualities and suggested treatment of all of the popular fish of North America, fresh water and salt—along with more than 100 recipes.

Perhaps no other food is so dependent on freshness for optimum enjoyment as fish. Beef or game or almost any other type of red meat may be improved by aging—that is, deliberately allowing the meat, under controlled conditions, to develop a flavor which is riper than that of the fresh meat. But with fish, the aim always is to maintain that delicate, fresh-caught taste; to prevent, if at all possible, even the slightest hint of ripeness.

Many kinds of fish, if properly frozen, can be eaten months after they are caught and still taste perfectly fresh. Yet the very same kinds might just as easily develop a disagreeably strong flavor only a day—even hours—after being pulled from the water. The difference, of course, lies in how well they are cared for.

All too many anglers, whether in haste or ignorance, take proper care of their catch at some stages between hook and table, but not at others. All steps are crucial. A fish that is tainted will not lose its rancidity in the freezer, no matter how well you wrap and store it. Nor will a fish gently handled on the water and lovingly carried home on a dry bed of ice be any more palatable a month later if sloppily frozen.

Oddly, a lot of fishermen who treat the handling of their fish quite casually show far too much concern about cooking. It's not unusual for a person to feel that every species of fish has its own special ways of being cooked, and must be prepared just-so. These misguided souls might spend hours looking up a recipe for, say, bluefish, after they have refused to spend five minutes making sure their catch is well-iced and drained for the drive home.

Anyone who follows the few simple procedures explained in the chapters on cooking should have little trouble making a tasty dish out of any fish he might catch—whether he can or can't find its name in any of the standard family cookbooks.

And with the more involved recipes offered here, it's not the fish that might be challenging to prepare, but what goes on it or in it.

For maximum usefulness of "From Hook to Table" it is suggested that you first look up your fish in the listing in Chapter Seven. There you will get *brief* suggestions on how to dress the fish and how best to cook it. Then you can consult Chapter Two for cleaning instructions in step-by-step detail, and from there go to Chapter Four for basic cooking procedures.

Almost always, there is a wide choice of possibilities for any food fish. It's up to you to decide whether you want simply fried, broiled or baked fish, or want to try one of the more than 100 recipes in Chapter Six.

For outdoor cooking, look at Chapter Five.

But for all that advice, you probably won't be happy with your meal unless you pay careful attention to the proper handling of your catch, as outlined in Chapters One and Three.

CHAPTER ONE:

ON THE WATER

Understandably, a fisherman's main concern while he's on the water is to catch fish. Any matter of less pressing import—even eating lunch—is apt to be postponed as long as possible, or at least as long as there are good-looking spots to be cast to and the angler is not too exhausted to lift his arm.

But in fishing, as in every other pursuit, there are necessary chores which demand attention. Time must be made for paddling and rigging and anchoring and sharpening hooks. And for the millions of fishermen who enjoy eating some of their fish almost as much as catching them, time must also be carefully devoted to the few small but vital requirements of proper care which will assure getting the catch home in a fresh and flavorful condition.

Angling is primarily a warm-weather sport, and so your immediate aim must be to hold down the natural rise in temperature of fish after they leave the water. Obviously, in those few cases where the air temperature is as low as, or lower than, the water temperature (ice fishing, for instance, or certain other kinds of winter fishing), the problem is not so serious, and may not exist at all; but in the overall fishing picture, such cases are far in the minority.

One good way to hold off deterioration is to keep the fish alive as long as possible. With most freshwater fish (notable exceptions being trout and salmon) and with many saltwater fish as well, the best way to keep them frisky is in a livewell with adequate aeration or recirculating water. Many boats now have built-in livewells that offer both decent capacity and adequate oxygenation. In fresh water this has been brought about by the bass tournaments—large and small, pro and amateur—which insist that the bass be kept alive and then released after weighing. During non-competitive trips, many bassers use the wells to keep alive a few small "eating size" bass or other table fish. In salt water, live-wells have become common on boats of all sizes for an entirely different reason—to hold live baits, some of which are quite large.

On smaller boats, or when fishing from shore, the angler can either string his fish and return them to the water, or else deposit them in a fish bag or basket which is held in the water, and be confident that they will remain frisky for some time.

STRINGERS

Stringers are available in two basic styles. One is simply a cord fitted at one end with a rigid point and at the other with a ring. With panfish, you can slip the point under the gill cover and out its mouth, taking care not to injure the gills. With bass and other larger catches, stick the point through both jaws of the fish. In either case, you then pull the stringer all the way through until the ring is just outside the gill. Now, by running the point through the ring and tightening it, you secure the first fish to the stringer. With all others, you simply run the point through gill and mouth.

The second common type is the chain stringer, which features individual safety-pin type clips for every fish you put on it. Though the chain stringer can be used for other species, it is most popular among bass fishermen—its eight or ten clips representing the daily bag limit for bass in most states. The best method for affixing a bass to one of the clips is to run the open point of the clip through both lips of the bass.

When stringing a fish you should handle it as little as possible and get the stringer into the water at once. Be sure that the other end of the stringer is firmly fastened to boat or bank. This may sound like unnecessary advice, and indeed it should be, but many an unhappy fisherman has lost a good string of fish through carelessness in this regard.

So long as the stringer remains submerged, your fish have a good chance of staying alive. But it's a rare angler who doesn't move from spot to spot during a day's fishing. Chances are your catch will survive short periods of transport lying on the deck, but if you anticipate a long haul, it's best to deposit the string in a pail of water. In either event, don't forget to put the stringer overside as soon as you stop.

A stringer can safely be left in the water while you paddle or slow-troll. As a matter of fact, slow movement undoubtedly adds to the stringer-life of your fish. But when you motor at even a medium speed, the stringer must be taken aboard.

Fish bags and baskets have the same function as stringers, their purpose being to keep your fish alive and in the water. Many rental boats are fitted with livewells, and while such wells are mainly for bait, your fish can be kept in them too, so long as they don't become overcrowded. Note, however, that not all livewells recirculate water copiously enough to keep larger fish alive for any great length of time.

Whether you use a stringer, bag or livewell, you must keep a steady check on your fish and quickly make other arrangements for any that die. Dead fish are apt to spoil more rapidly in the water than out of it.

It's a good idea to remove any casualties from stringer or bag at once. If you don't have an ice chest, simply put them in a shady spot where there is free circulation of air, or cover them loosely with a damp rag or some other vegetation. The dampness will help keep them cool by evaporation, and also helps prevent the surface drying that would make them more difficult to dress later on.

ICE CHESTS

Anyone who fishes from a boat that doesn't have built-in coolers should by all means take along a portable ice chest and a supply of ice. Coolers are now available in such an array of sizes and prices that there's no problem finding one that can conveniently be lugged along in even the smallest boat. Nor is it much trouble to carry along a cooler when you fish from dock or bridge. Folks who do their fishing afoot obviously cannot lug along a box of ice, but unless it's only a short drive home, they should at least keep an ice chest in the car.

The surest and easiest method for taking care of a fresh-caught fish is to deposit it directly in an ice chest. Thereafter, the only thing to worry about until time to dress your catch is that the box stays reasonably well drained, and, of course, that it remains shut except when you must put something in or take something out.

Often, however, it is impractical to carry along an ice chest for the exclusive purpose of holding your catch. One

Author's son Dan hoists a banner family stringer of bluegills, the nation's favorite panfish.

chest may have to serve double duty as a repository for cold drinks, and in this case you still make effective use of a stringer. Keep your fish on the stringer so long as they remain frisky, but if a fish dies, transfer it to the ice chest. To avoid contact with your drinks or lunch, place the fish in a plastic bag first. Or keep your lunch in a tight container, and don't worry about the drinks. A rinse and a wipe will remove all traces of fishy taste or aroma from bottle or can.

At trip's end, of course, you put all your fish on ice for the ride home. However, if you prefer to dress your fish before leaving the waterside, here are a few other pointers which should be followed.

With dressed fish, special care should be taken to make sure that the fish are not allowed to sit in water which has melted from the ice. Fish flesh that comes into direct contact with water—even ice water—can quickly become soft and unappetizing. Drain the chest thoroughly before packing your dressed fish. And if you have to drive a long way, plan one or more stops to drain the chest enroute.

With filleted fish, rather than fish which are merely scaled and gutted, it is even more important to keep them dry in the ice chest, preferably by using plastic bags. If plastic bags aren't available, cover the ice with several thicknesses of newspaper and place the fillets on top.

TROUT AND SALMON

It has been mentioned that trout and salmon need special care. The proper handling of those fish seems almost ritualistic, yet the ritual is a practical one, designed to keep these delicate table species at their peak of appearance and flavor.

If you are going to keep some of these fish for your table, they should be killed quickly with a blow on the head or, in the case of smaller specimens, by breaking the back just behind the head with your hands. Ideally, the fish should then be dressed at once, but chances are you're anxious to cast again. So lay the fish aside and dress it at the very first break. The fish should be placed in a creel of wicker or mesh (so air can circulate), or else placed in a shady spot in the boat or on the bank.

As soon as you can get to it, slit the fish and remove the entrails and gills, as well as the blood-line lying along the backbone (the procedure is illustrated in Chapter Two). The fish should then be wrapped in a dry rag, or day grass, and returned to the creel. Naturally, you don't put king-sized salmon in a creel, but you still dress as soon as possible, then keep them in a cool and *dry* place.

Part of the ritual, with small trout especially, is to keep individual fish from coming into contact with each other, since any point of contact will result in a blemish. It doesn't harm the taste or texture—just the sensitivity of some trout fishermen.

The reason trout and salmon are killed so quickly is to prevent their flapping around, with resultant damage to the surface appearance. A lot of people refer to such damage as "bruises" and swear that every bruise impugns the flavor. It really isn't likely that the quality of the fish is harmed by bumps and jolts, but the appearance definitely is and to many that is a goodly part of a trout dinner.

On the other hand, there is no debate about the effect of water on a dressed trout. If the trout must be washed, rinse it lightly and wipe at once. Preferably, you should not wash, but wipe with a damp rag to remove any foreign substances.

Trout and salmon which are put on ice should be even more carefully bagged or wrapped than other species.

CHAPTER TWO:

FISH CLEANING AND DRESSING

Perhaps cleaning fish will never be looked upon as one of man's great recreational delights, but at least the task becomes less objectionable if three basic rules are followed: (1) keep the right tools handy; (2) clean the fish in a place selected for maximum ease and convenience; (3) familiarize yourself with any of the different cleaning techniques you're likely to need—and practice them.

Often the only tool needed is a knife, but it must be a good one—and sharp. Traditionally, the most useful all-around tool has been a fillet knife with six-inch blade, but the electric knife that has come along in recent years will win most fish-cleaning contests by a mile. So popular have the electrics become that many marinas and fishing camps now provide outlets for plugging them in at cleaning tables. Rechargeable electric knives—along with 12-volt models that plug into the cigarette lighter of your boat or car—come to the rescue in places where there is no electricity or no convenient plug.

Back to standard knives. Many models are available on fishing tackle counters, and with stainless blades they range in price from a few dollars to out-of-sight—the really expensive ones being hand-crafted. Just any good knife won't do for efficient filleting. While some kitchen knives may look similar, a proper fillet knife has a blade that is thinner and not so rigid as, say, a boning knife. Opinions vary among anglers as to just how flexible the filleting blade should be, but some degree of flexibility is a must.

The most common blade length for fillet knives is six inches. Four-inch blades (or pocket knives) will be needed at times for dressing panfish, and eight- or nine-inch blades are the ticket for saltwater anglers who sometimes have to tangle with bigger catches, such as grouper.

It's advisable to keep one six-inch fillet knife in your tackle kit, and an identical one at home. And it's not a bad idea to keep *two* in the tackle box. That's in case your fishing buddy, at cleaning time, announces that he's "forgotten" to bring along a knife of his own. Think how pleased he'll be when you graciously offer him the use of your spare!

Other cleaning tools which may well come in handy—depending on where you fish, and for what—are a scaler and a pair of pliers.

And it almost goes without saying that a sharpening stone should always be close at hand. Again, try to keep one in your tackle box and another at home, for those times when you're unable to clean your fish on the water.

Obviously, you could drag your tools out of the tackle box for home cleaning, which would be perfectly all right so long as you're the infallible type who always remembers to put them back. Unfortunately, I'm not. Nor are any of my fishing pals.

But cleaning fish at home should basically be avoided if at all possible. A waterside table saves as much time and effort as the right tools. Most marinas and fish camps do provide fish-cleaning facilities—a table or wooden surface of the appropriate height, complete with handy water supply. But even without those, you'll normally find it easier to clean fish on location than to bring them home and do it.

Fish scales fly hither and yon as you scrape them off, and your wife may take a dim view of scales speckling her kitchen. Also, there is a disposal problem in the average city home.

But if you *must* dress your fish at home, here are some hints that should help. When scaling, hold the fish under water in the sink, so the scales won't fly about. Then, for gutting and beheading, place numerous thicknesses of newspaper on a counter top. As the mess grows, keep wrapping it in a few layers of paper and setting it aside. This not only avoids a single big pile of garbage, but also provides you with a new and clean surface from time to time as you go along. When you're filleting instead of dressing and scaling, place the pad of newspaper sheets atop a cutting board and, again, wrap the refuse at intervals as you find necessary.

As each fish (or fillet) leaves the cleaning surface, it should be placed, without rinsing, in a dry sink or dry, clean pail. Wait until the entire job is finished, before you rinse all the dressed fish under cold running water and then immediately prepare them for cold-storing or freezing as described in Chapter Three.

Several factors must be considered in determining how you wish to dress your fish. One of them, obviously, is size. You wouldn't try to stuff and bake an average-size bluegill. The selected method of cooking is another important consideration. When you bring home a redfish, say, or a red snapper, or a four-pound bass, you'll have a decision to make: Should you prepare the fish whole for baking, or remove the fillets for frying or broiling?

Such fish as large salmon and king mackerel are normally steaked. But in smaller sizes, they could be either steaked or filleted, according to your own preference.

Once you make a choice as to the end product desired, proceed with the task of dressing, as described in the illustrated instructions which follow.

DRESSING PANFISH

"Panfish" is a catchall term for any edible fish, whether from fresh water or the sea, which is so small that it is normally cooked nearly whole. Naturally, the entrails must be removed, and usually, but not always, the head is lopped off as well. Some people prefer to leave the head on for visual appeal; others maybe because there are a few bites of exceptionally tasty meat in the "cheeks" of many fish. If the head is not removed, the gills should be cut out. The majority of panfish also require scaling, but with a few—such as small freshwater trout and saltwater pompano, scales are either non-existent or small enough to be ignored. The list of edible fish in this book makes note of those kinds which need no scaling, but if any doubt persists, it really won't hurt any of them to undergo a scraping.

1. Since you'll usually be dressing a lot of panfish at once, you should use a scaling device that's fast and efficient. The patented scaler shown here is excellent, and some other good ones are available in stores. Or you can use a knife (preferably dull) or a spoon—whatever suits you best.

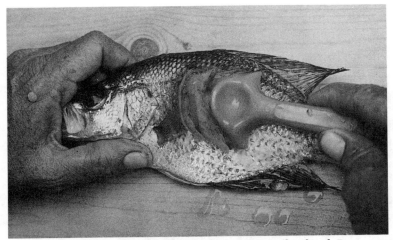

2. You scale, of course, "against the grain" or from tail to head. Be sure to get the scales that are close under the dorsal and anal fins.

3. Pay extra attention to the spots that might be overlooked if you get in too big a hurry—top and bottom surfaces forward of the tail, as shown, and the "throat" area.

4. Cut off the head. Some like to cut the pectoral fins off with it, as shown. Others prefer to cut closer behind the gills and leave the pectorals.

5. Slit the belly and remove the entrails.

6. The panfish is now ready for the pan. The dorsal and anal fins could be cut out (see how in *Preparing a Large Fish for Baking*), but this takes considerably more time and is not really necessary, because the fins are easily removed after cooking. See "How to Eat Panfish," Chapter Five.

DRESSING PANFISH, HAND-HELD

Here's an alternate system for dressing panfish when no cleaning table or flat surface is available. Use it at streamside or lakeside when preparing fish for a shore lunch or camp dinner.

1. Hold fish in hand and, with the blade of a pocket knife held vertically, scrape off the scales. Turn fish over and scrape the other side. Take care to remove the scales from top and bottom surfaces. Since scales flake from most panfish without much effort, you are not apt to cut yourself, but you obviously must be careful.

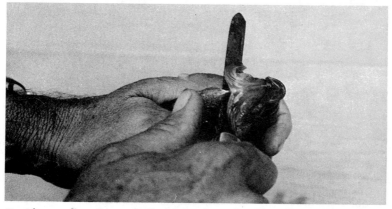

2. After scaling, insert knife blade through gills and cut through the "throat" connection.

3. Cut off the head, including gills. You can now remove the entrails by making a slit in the belly cavity, or by inserting a finger into the cavity from the front and pulling them out.

4. Rinse well and panfish is ready for mealing and frying.

PREPARING FISH FOR BAKING

Procedures for dressing a large fish that you plan to bake are essentially the same as for panfish. But it's a bigger job, of course, and one that will require more effort and more elbow room.

In addition to scaling and eviscerating the fish, you may wish to remove the dorsal and anal fins as well, because this will eliminate many small bones that would prove troublesome after the fish reaches the serving platter.

In removing the fins, take care to follow the directions shown here, so that all the little bones come with them. Otherwise, why bother at all? Simply slicing off the fins at the surface serves no purpose except to make the fish look a little neater. As a final step, you may also cut off the tail, but there is no real reason to do so unless it doesn't fit your pan.

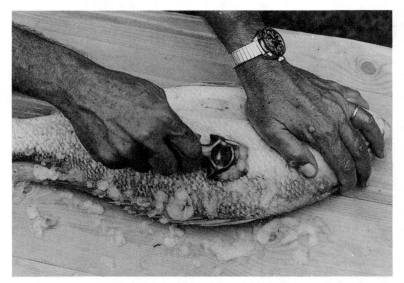

1. The first step is to scale the fish. This can be a pretty tough job with many species. Again, my preferred tool is the same patented scaler I use for panfish, although a sturdy tablespoon will do the trick. As with panfish, take care that all scales are removed from dorsal and belly surfaces, as well as from the sides.

2. Remove the head. Some like to leave the head on for dramatic effect, and if you prefer to do so, be sure to cut out the gills. It is difficult to slice through the backbone of a large fish. It may be easier for you if you first cut through the "throat," as shown in the picture, then grasp the head from the underside and pull it upward to break the spine. The knife should then cut through easily.

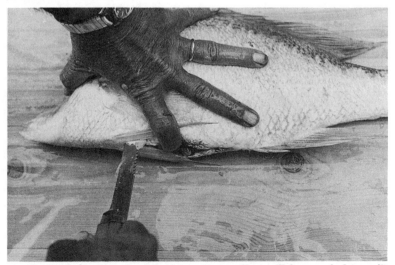

3. Slit the belly from vent to throat. Extra effort will be needed to split the fin.

4. Remove entrails and scrape blood pockets from spine area.

5. At this stage, the fish could be ready. The dorsal and anal fins can be left on and pulled out after cooking, but some bones might be left, so it's best to take just a little more time and remove them.

6. Keeping knife flat, make a rather deep cut the length of the dorsal fin. Turn fish and make the same cut along the other side of the dorsal.

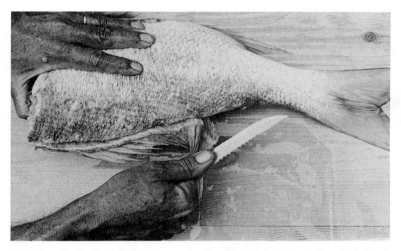

7. Using the knife to help grip, grasp the dorsal fish at the tail end and pull firmly upward and toward the head end. You may have to stop and get a new grip once or twice. The fin and all connecting bones will come out.

8. Repeat steps 6 and 7 with the smaller anal fin on the underside, and your fish is ready for stuffing and baking. No need to remove the other fins (pectoral and ventral) since these are attached to large rigid bones rather than troublesome small ones.

DRESSING TROUT AND SALMON

These fish should be field-dressed as soon as they're caught, or very shortly thereafter, in the following manner:

1. Make a slit the entire length of the belly from vent to gills.

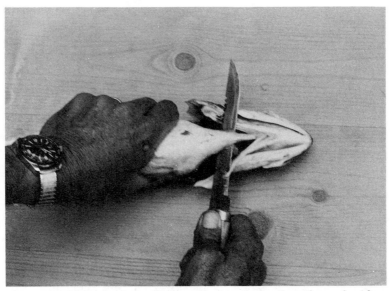

2. Cut the "throat" where gills are joined to the head on the underside.

3. Remove entrails and cut out the gills.

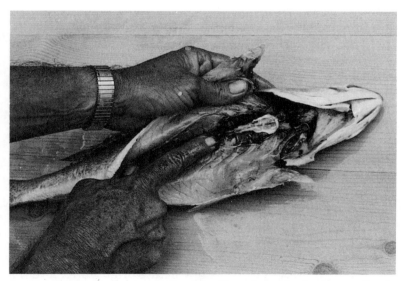

4. With forefinger, work out the bloodline along the backbone. Trout should now be wiped clean. Trout scales are so small they can be ignored. Therefore, this field-dressing is all that's needed. Of course, with larger trout and most salmon, you will wish to steak or fillet them before cooking.

STEAKING

In fish-eating lexicon, a "steak" usually means a slice cut from the dressed carcass of a whole fish, with a segment of backbone included. The term is also applied, however, to slices cut from the boneless fillets of very large fish, such as swordfish. Steaks vary in thickness from a minimum of about a half-inch to as much as two inches. The average is around three quarters of an inch.

When should a fish be steaked rather than filleted? There's no rigid rule on this, but these tips may help you decide.

(1) Follow custom. Many market fish—halibut, large salmon, king mackerel and swordfish among them—are usually sold as steaks, so anglers often follow the same custom with their own catches.

(2) Appearance. You may just like the looks of a broiled fish steak on your plate better than a fillet, or partial fillet, cut from the same fish.

(3) Variable size capability. You can slice fish steaks to preferred thicknesses—using thin teaks for quick cooking or fatter ones for slower cooking methods, especially with recipes that include sauces or special trimmings.

(4) The most common reason for steaking is simply that the particular fish is too large to make filleting practical. But in this case, of course, you have a good option: Instead of steaking the entire "log" of the fish, you can cut the thick fillets from both sides of the backbone and then cut half-size steaks from the fillets.

To prepare a whole fish for steaking you can essentially follow the same instructions as for preparing a baking fish. The first step is scaling—if necessary. This step can be eliminated with members of the mackerel and salmon families. Next, eviscerate the fish and cut off the head.

Again, it's your choice as to whether or not to remove the dorsal and anal fins. Fish markets generally leave them intact, both to save labor and to keep each steak more attractive. If you cut out the fins before steaking, the steaks will be

Steaking a fish is almost like thick-slicing a loaf of bread.

joined in the middle but split at the top, and some of them at the bottom too—not so pretty but less bony.

With the carcass lying on a cutting board, make a straight-down cut, very much like slicing a loaf of bread. Of course, there is no backbone in a loaf of bread, and the spine may cause you some trouble, depending on the size of your fish, its species and what tools you have.

Sometimes, with fairly small or soft-boned fish, your knife will slice right through the bone with little effort— and with big fish too, if you happen to hit between the verte-brae. If the bone resists your knife, don't struggle. Simply cut through the flesh until you hit the bone, then take care of the bone with a kitchen saw, frozen food knife or a cleaver. Or, if your knife is thick-bladed and sturdy, you can hammer it through.

Near the tail end of the carcass, your steaks may get too small to bother with. You can either preserve the remaining tail-end portion in one chunk for baking, or you can fillet the remaining meat from both sides of the bone—just like fillet-ing a whole fish.

HOW TO FILLET AND SKIN, SYSTEM 1

This is the easiest and fastest of all fish-cleaning methods, and one that's suitable for the great majority of catches, large or small. The product is two slabs of boneless, or nearly boneless, flesh from each fish. Both skin and scales are most often removed simultaneously but, if you prefer, you can scale the fish before filleting it and leave the skin on. That's up to you. Skin may add something to the taste of certain species, but in some others it imparts a disagreeable flavor. Consult the "Guide to Hook and Line Table Fish," Chapter Seven, for suggestions, but remember that even in species which don't really require it, removing the skin means only a slightly milder flavor.

Many fishermen may never think of filleting any fish under, say, one pound in weight, but many others routinely fillet their larger bluegills or species that normally are treated as panfish. The fillets will be quite small, of course, but if you have a great many of them—enough, at least, to feed the number of people you have in mind—they are delicious and, best of all, boneless.

Exceptionally large bluegills or other sunfish that are caught from still or muddy water may have a strong "musky" flavor, much like that of largemouth bass from the same water. Filleting and skinning will remove the flavor, most of which can be traced to fat just under the skin.

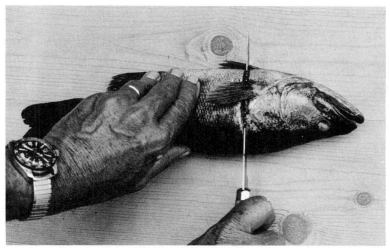

1. Place whole fish on firm surface. With sharp, fairly flexible fillet knife, make a cut straight down, just behind the pectoral fin and all the way to the backbone.

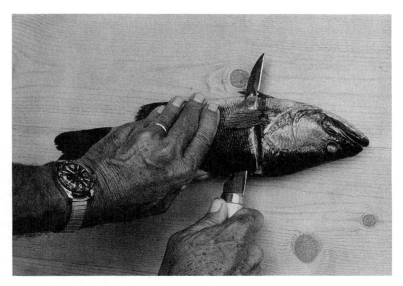

2. Turn the knife until its blade is flat against the backbone, with its edge pointing toward the tail. Keeping knife flat, work toward the tail with a slight sawing motion.

3. You'll cut through the rib bones, leaving the chest cavity with the fillet. Usually, the entrails stay clear of the chest cavity, but this isn't important at the moment.

4. Here's the carcass, with both fillets removed. If you wish, you can now cut off the head, discard the entrails and keep the backbone for frying or for making stock.

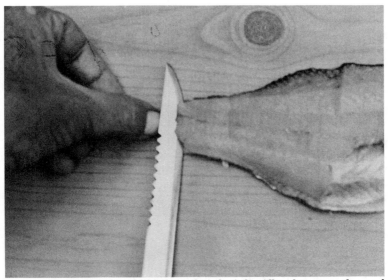

5. To separate the skin, hold the tail end of the fillet down snugly—and work the knife edge forward until the blade lies nearly flat between skin and flesh, but with the edge angled slightly downward. Too much of a downward angle and you might cut through the skin. But if the blade angles a little bit upward, you may lose some good meat. Sounds like a tougher challenge than it really is. You should soon get the hang of it.

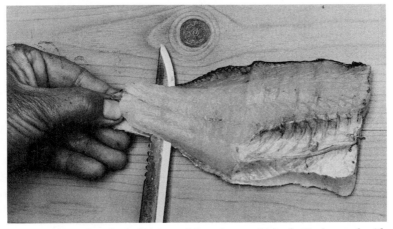

6. With the tail-end of skin in a tight grip, work the knife forward with a scissoring motion while simultaneously pulling on the skin with the other hand. The pulling is as important as the cutting to an efficient skinning job.

7. Properly done, very little meat will be left on the skin.

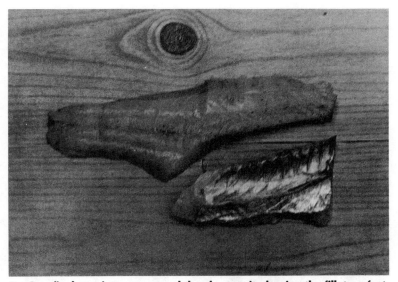

8. One final step is to cut around the chest cavity, leaving the fillet perfectly boneless. Most people prefer it this way, but folks who don't mind picking out bones leave the rib cage intact. The number and location of small bones around the rib cage varies from species to species, so feel along the cut edge with your finger, as more trimming may be necessary. With some species, such as East Coast sheepshead and the other kinds of porgies, additional bones are found along the center line that runs from the rib cage toward the tail. Feel these with your fingers and cut them out by slicing above and below the center line for an inch or so behind the rib-cage cut.

HOW TO SKIN AND FILLET, SYSTEM 2

The end result of this method is the same as that of the preceding system—a pair of boneless fillets. The only difference in treatment is that the order is reversed. You remove the skin first, then cut off the fillets.

Why another system for doing the same thing? Mainly because there are some types of fish—dolphin being the most prominent—which just don't surrender their hides smoothly or easily after the fillets are removed.

And, of course, there is personal preference, Many anglers like to do it this way with bass and other fish.

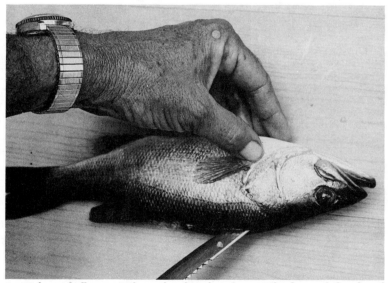

1. Make a shallow cut along the dorsal surface at the base of the dorsal fin. Run the cut from immediately in back of the head to just forward of the tail.

2. Make a shallow cut diagonally, from the forward end of the dorsal cut to a point on the underside near the vent. Then make a third cut from that point to just forward of the tail on the underside.

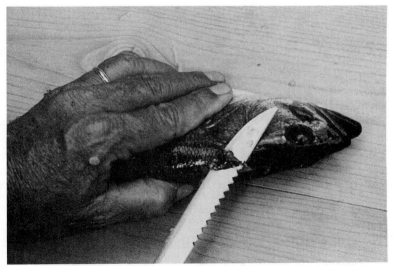

3. Use the knife blade to pry up a triangle of skin where the two cuts meet behind the head.

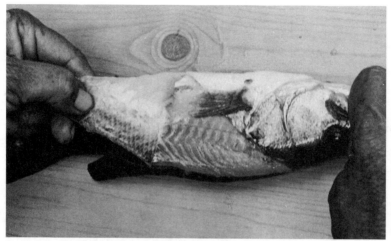

4. Grasp the flap of skin between thumb and finger. Holding the head firmly with your other hand, peel off the skin. With larger fish, it may help to use the knife blade as a backup for your thumb in getting a firm grip on the skin. Or, of course, you can use pliers.

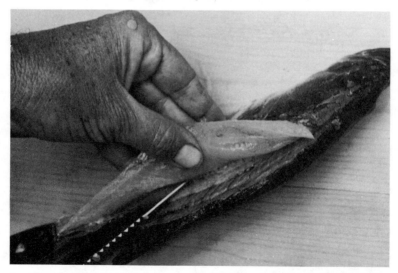

5. After the skin is peeled away, cut closely against the backbone, lifting the fillet as you proceed. You can cut around the rib cage, leaving it intact and still attached to he carcass. Or you can slice off the whole fillet, ribs included, and trim the bones away afterwards, as in the preceding system.

Poppy Brownlee has dinner plans for her dolphin. But first, it will have to be skinned and then filleted—not vice versa.

THE DOUBLE FILLET

Both fillets from the same fish can be left attached on the underside, providing a double fillet, sometimes called a "butterfly" fillet.

There are several common uses for a double fillet. One is planking—that is, tacking or pinning the meat to a wooden plank or shingle, skin side down, then propping the shingle at the edge of an open fire for campfire broiling.

Many like the double fillet for home use too. They spread a stuffing atop one side, fold the other side over it and bake. The same thing could be done with two separate fillets—and often is—but I suppose there is a certain amount of *chic* involved. Also, the double fillet leaves the skin intact, and this helps improve the baked product by holding in juices.

If preparing a double fillet for home baking, the first step is to scale the fish. For planked fish at the campfire, scaling is unnecessary because the scales and skin will remain fixed to the plank. You just fork the meat away from the skin into your plate or mess kit.

1. **After scaling, cut off the head just behind the pectoral fin.**

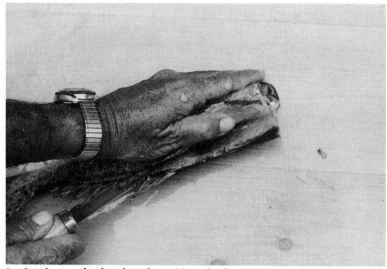

2. Starting at the head end, position the knife flat against the backbone and cut toward the rear—slicing through the rib bones but taking care not to cut through the skin on the belly. When you reach the vent, however, push the knife point through the bottom skin and finish cutting off the fillet to the tail.

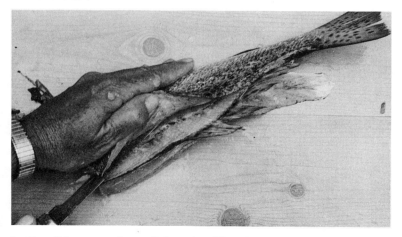

3. Turn fish over and cut off the other fillet. This time you'll probably find it easier to start at the tail end. Cut through from top to bottom until you reach the vent, then make sure the knife point stays inside the chest cavity while you slice through the ribs and complete the filleting.

4. This is the double fillet, ready for stuffing and baking. After discarding the entrails, the backbone may also be kept for frying if you like.

FILLETING EXTRA-LARGE FISH

If a fish "fits the knife," then cutting off the fillets is no big problem. But with unusually large fish you'll have to go about things just a little differently. One obvious approach is simply to use a longer knife. Another is to cut as far as you can with the short knife blade, then lift the cut portion up and away from the backbone with your opposite hand as you make succeedingly deeper cuts until, finally, you get all the way through.

Now, of course, the fillet is still too wide to permit skinning in the usual manner. Attack this problem, as shown in the illustrations, by converting the large fillet into two or more narrower ones before skinning.

Another choice is to use Filleting System No. 2—removing the skin before you remove the fillets. However, with most large fish the following approach is much easier.

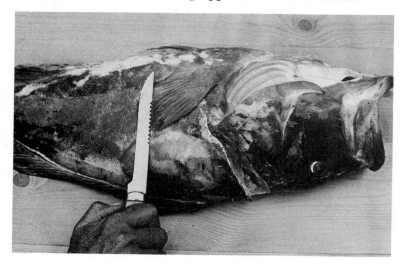

1. Note that the fillet is wider than the knife blade is long—meaning that you won't be able to slice it off with one continuous stroke. Instead, make a straight-down cut to the backbone just behind the head then, with the knife blade flattened alongside the backbone, slice as deeply as you can, all the way to the tail.

2. Lift the fillet and continue slicing it away from the bone. Again, you have your choice of working around the rib cage or slicing through it. With large fish, it will take a sturdy knife and considerable effort to cut the ribs.

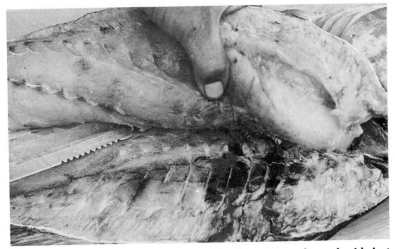

3. Continue lifting and slicing until you reach the skin on the underside just behind the rib cage. Then cut through that skin and complete the filleting.

4. Now, of course, the fillet is still too wide to allow skinning in the manner described in System No. 1. So . . .

5. . . . you simply make the fillet "fit the knife" by cutting it in half lengthwise, along the center line.

6. Now each half can be skinned as if it were a single fillet.

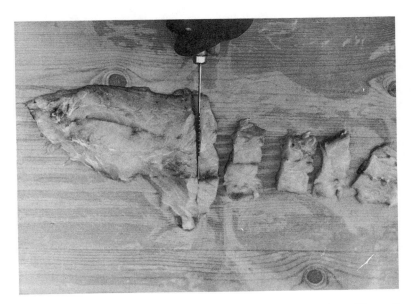

7. The final step is to cut each half into serving size pieces. Here, "fingers" are being sliced away for deep-frying. Or, you can leave the whole section intact for broiling or baking.

SKINNING CATFISH

Catfish should always be skinned, whether they're of pan-fish size or lunkers which must afterwards be filleted or chunked. The skin is tough but thin and slippery, and so the procedure is different from those used for scaly fishes. You can manage the skinning job by holding the fish in your hands, but the following way is the best of all, by far.

1. An ordinary board with a nail driven through it at an angle will make the job of skinning catfish far easier—especially if you have a lot of them to clean.

2. Make a cut through the skin from one side, across the top, to the other side, just back of the head.

3. Impale the head of the fish on the nail. This is best done by grabbing the fish well back of the head and "hammering" the head against the nail. Now grasp the skin at the cut with pliers and pull toward the tail.

4. The skin usually will come off in one piece. Sometimes, however, it will separate along the dorsal surface. This means only that you'll have to grip and pull a second time.

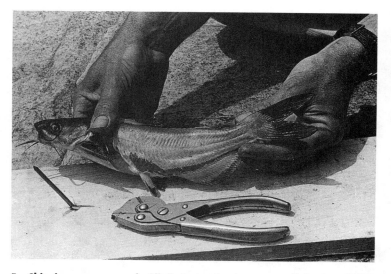

5. Skin is now removed. All that remains is to cut off the head, slit the belly and remove the entrails. If a small strip of skin remains on the belly, pull it off with pliers before slitting. Small catfish can be fried whole. Larger ones are easily filleted after skinning.

Channel catfish, whether pan-size or fillet size like this one make welcome table fare for anglers everywhere.

HOW TO BONE SHAD

Shad roe is a famous delicacy. So is shad—even though all too many anglers, if they keep the fish, end up discarding it or giving it away because they don't want to battle the little bones that are scattered through the flesh in apparent helter-skelter fashion. But the arrangement isn't really unfathomable at all. And, yes, there is a way to get rid of the bones. Here it is:

1. Slit the belly carefully to avoid puncturing the roe. Remove the roe and entrails. Scale the shad and cut off the head.

2. To remove the fillet, start by working the knife through the skin along the length of the dorsal surface.

3. Lift up the fillet and continue cutting close to the backbone. Again, you can either let the knife slide over the top of the rib cage, or you can cut through the ribs and trim them away later.

4. Lay the fillet skin side down. The "extra" bones in a shad fillet are located in two rows, each running the length of the fillet about an inch on either side of the center line. To get at these bones, make a lengthwise cut about one-half inch from the center line on either side.

5. Insert the knife point in one of the lengthwise cuts and work it underneath the bones, prying up slightly until you can get a grip on the bones with your finger.

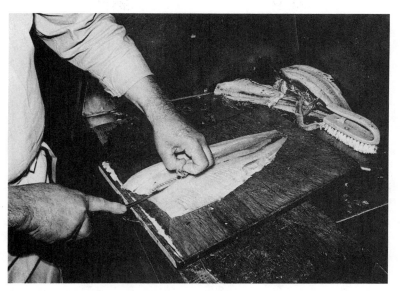

6. Now pull gently, while trimming a path with the knife bit by bit. Shortly you'll work the entire length of bone out of the fillet.

7. But don't forget that each fillet has *two* strips of bone. Go to the other side of the center line and work the second set of bones out in the same manner. The fillet is now boneless and ready for broiling.

CHAPTER THREE:

COLD-STORING AND FREEZING FISH

As soon as you get home from a fishing trip, you should make sure that your fish are taken care of before doing any other chores. Even before you wash the boat or sit down to dinner, the least you should do is check the ice chest. If plenty of ice is left, and proper drainage seen to, you can safely postpone refrigerating or freezing—perhaps even until the following morning. Just be sure there is enough ice to last (or add more), and open the drain plug.

Should you wish to keep fish for several days without freezing them, you can manage it in either of two ways. A small amount of fish can be wrapped and stored in the coldest part of your refrigerator for two or three days—particularly in a covered meat keeper where the temperature is not apt to drop drastically with frequent opening of the refrigerator door. If you're trying to hold a larger quantity of

DRAIN YOUR ICE CHEST: Water should be drained from the ice chest regularly when fish are being stored or transported inside. Especially with dressed fish, water contact causes loss of color and flavor, and also imparts a mushy texture to the flesh. Even if you use plastic bags, water can enter through faulty seals or tiny punctures and reduce the quality of your fish.

fish than the refrigerator can efficiently accommodate, keep them in your portable ice chest, well wrapped and well iced.

But remember that the chest must be checked every few hours. If you're away at work, assign the chore to someone else once or twice during the day. A modern chest, well-insulated with plastic foam, will probably hold the ice well for several hours, anyway—depending on the ratio of fish to ice which it contains. The scheduled checks, however, are as much for drainage as for ice supply. It's common for the drain to get stopped up. So run a pencil or screwdriver blade into the drain at every check to assure that there's no blockage.

Personally, I prefer to freeze my fish, even if I plan on using them within a few days.

For different reasons, fish kept either in a refrigerator or an ice chest must be protected with an air-tight or water-tight cover. In the refrigerator, uncovered fish dries out so rapidly that it can begin losing quality within an hour or so. Long contact with water, on the other hand, tends to make the flesh soft and robs it of flavor—hence the constant harping on plastic bags and drainage for iced fish.

I seldom refrigerate fresh fish unless I plan to cook it the next day. Then I cut it into frying-size pieces and hold the pieces overnight in a sealed bag in the refrigerator. Or I might put the pieces in a bowl, and cover the bowl with plastic wrap. Or, if it is a large fish which I plan to bake, I will wrap the whole thing in foil or heavy freezer paper—as carefully as I would for freezing.

TO HOLD IN REFRIGERATOR: When dressed and ready for the table, fish may be held in the refrigerator for perhaps three days without losing quality—so long as they are well covered to prevent dehydration. Cover refrigerated fish, even if you plan to cook it in a few hours. Large fish can be wrapped in freezer paper, as for freezing. Small portions can be placed in a bowl and covered with plastic wrap. Take care to seal the wrap around the edge of the bowl.

HOW TO FREEZE FISH

When properly packaged and kept in a freezer which can be depended upon to freeze them quickly and keep them frozen solidly, many kinds of fish can be kept for a year—and they still taste fresh when served.

Such long-term freezing can be accomplished with the lean types of fish, characterized by firm, white meat, and little or no red or dark streaks. Examples include freshwater bass and panfish, saltwater grouper, snook, flounder and many others.

Fat or oily fishes, such as mackerel, bluefish, mullet and salmon do not have nearly so long a freezer life, because the oils in the flesh tend to go rancid. Until I hit upon the coffee-can freezing method, which will be described shortly, I found that mullet and mackerel developed a rancid taste in the freezer within a week or two. But now I enjoy them up to three months after freezing.

If you're not sure whether a particular kind of fish is lean or fat, the rule of thumb is that the fat ones usually have an obviously dark-tinted flesh—pink in the case of salmon and trout; grayish or reddish in the mackerels, bluefish and most tunas.

As mentioned above, the meat of lean fish is white, although there may be patches of red. Even with these, best freezing results will be obtained if you trim away the red parts, as these are blood streaks which may go rancid.

Nearly every angler knows that fish should be wrapped well before freezing in order to avoid drying out (called "freezer burn"). Dried spots are not harmful, but the dried areas themselves are tough and tasteless, and when you see spots of freezer-burn, you can be almost sure that the rest of the fish will have, at best, an "unfresh" taste.

The very best way of protecting fish from freezer burn is to freeze them within a block of ice. And there are refinements even here. Long ago, I used to put fish in a metal loaf-cake pan, fill the pan with water, freeze the whole thing, and then remove the frozen block, wrap it in freezer paper and return it to the freezer. Later I graduated to plastic-coated milk cartons—depositing fillets or panfish therein, filling with water and folding down the top. This was a great improvement, but neither procedure is nearly so handy, fast or completely protective as the device I now use—a metal coffee can.

In my household there is seldom a shortage of coffee cans, and we even have them in two sizes, since we buy regular coffee in two-pound containers, and decaffeinated coffee in the one-pound can.

If you're a fish-loving angler who drinks instant coffee, it's worth going back to home-brewed just to get the cans. I have found that, in addition to their sheer convenience, they keep frozen fish fresh-tasting far longer than any other container or wrap.

Two reasons undoubtedly contribute to the long freezer life. First, freezing takes place much faster because of the metal's conductivity. Second, the fish is doubly guarded—by solid metal and by ice—from the punctures, tearing and other accidents which might occur to introduce exposure of the flesh with resulting freezer-burn or deterioration.

Of course, you could use any can or plastic container of appropriate size, and many food items (margarine and cheese spreads, for example) now come in handy containers with the plastic snap-on lids that once were found only on the coffee cans. An advantage to the coffee can is that it needs only a quick rinse before it is ready for use as a freezing container, whereas packages that contained other products would have to be thoroughly washed.

You probably wonder if the cans will rust. This is not much of a problem, because all air is forced from the inside of the can when it is filled with water, and the outside is exposed only to dry, cold air: in short, not a corrosive atmosphere. And the can, of course, is plated. A little rust may develop after extended storage, but the ice surrounding the fish protects it from any flavor-altering exposure.

I find coffee cans most useful for small pieces of fish, cut up for frying. As to quantity, you may have to experiment a little, but generally the one-pound can holds enough such pieces for four or five people; the two-pound size enough for six or eight, perhaps even ten.

Drop the pieces loosely into the can. Do not pack them tightly, although you may shake the can to settle the pieces and perhaps make room for one or two more. Leave enough room at the top so that water can cover all the fish and still leave a little room for expansion of the ice as it freezes.

Fill the can with water from the cold tap. Let it sit a few seconds until all air bubbles disappear, then add more water, if necessary, to reach the desired level—about a half-inch below the lip.

Now all that's left is to snap on the lid and freeze. Use a black felt marker to write the contents and the date of freezing on the lid.

Small whole fillets and small panfish also fit well into the cans—especially the two-pound cans. Fillets from large fish can be rolled up loosely and fitted inside. Fish steaks often stack up very neatly in the two-pound container.

I discard the cans and their lids after one use as a freezing container.

FREEZING IN CANS: Cover with water for longest freezer life.

HOW MUCH IS A MESS?

Freezing just enough fish to make a meal for your family is a difficult task. Even a one-pound coffee can will hold more than enough fillets or steaks for many families, so you may be faced with a choice: Should you try to gauge how much fish to put into the can for a single meal? Or should you go ahead and pack it to capacity, with the idea either of holding it for a fish fry or a dinner with guests? In the name of freezer space, efficiency and economy, the full can should win. If you thaw a can of fish and find you have too much for supper, remember that leftover fish is usually delicious— and that there are many outstanding recipes for leftover fish in Chapter Six.

But there's also a way to keep some of your frozen fish available in small quantities. All you need to pull this off is a freezer with a shelf large enough to hold a cookie sheet. Wet your fillets thoroughly and put them on the cookie sheet in a single layer, sides not touching. Freeze the fillets solid and then repack them in a coffee can, plastic container or freezer-weight plastic bag. The pieces will stay separate and you can thaw only enough for one person if need be.

Any whole fish, large steak or other configuration too big to fit a can must, of course, be wrapped separately for freezing.

By far the best wrapping material is heavy-duty wrapping paper, plastic-coated on one side. Light plastic wrap, plastic bags and aluminum foil are other possibilities. Foil is well suited for the job, but punctures easily if your foods get shuffled around in the freezer.

Naturally, if you intend to eat the fish within a few days, you can use any of the airtight wraps. A puncture or two is not likely to cause freezer burn. But for long storage the heavy paper is best.

To wrap fish properly, tear off a piece of freezer paper large enough to cover the length and breadth with considerable overlap. Proceed as shown in the illustrations by bringing the sides together atop the fish and folding down several times until snug.

After you have wrapped the ends, it's a good idea to seal them with tape to prevent loosening later.

A grease pencil can be used to mark paper or foil, so long as the surface is not wet. Some felt markers will work even on a damp surface.

If you are freezing fish in plastic bags, it's all too easy to trap air inside when you seal the bag—which is the very thing you're trying to avoid by wrapping it up in the first place. To prevent this, hold the mouth of the bag open after putting in the fish, and dip the whole works into a sink or pail of water. Water pressure will force air out of the bag. Zip or twist the bag closed just above the surface.

If freezing fillets, the plastic bag may be filled with water before zipping or twisting it closed. The merits of freezing fish in water already have been noted, and while the bag may not offer as much protection as a can or plastic container, it is a fine second choice for fillets. Plastic bags come in a variety of weights (thicknesses). Choose those that are marketed especially for freezing foods.

WRAPPING FISH FOR FREEZING: Whole fish, big fillets or steaks too large to fit in a coffee can must be carefully wrapped with suitable material in order to be kept as air-tight as possible. Heavy-duty freezer paper, plasticized on one side, is the best material. Heavy aluminum foil is fine but can be punctured in a crowded freezer—allowing entry of air and subsequent dry spots called "freezer burn." Whatever wrapping material you choose, the procedure is the same.

1. Use a sheet large enough to allow plenty of overlap at both ends and at the top.

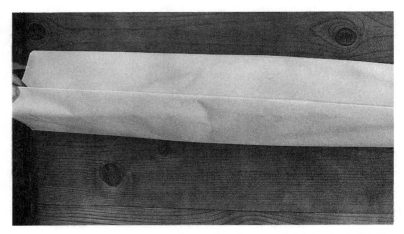

2. Bring the two top edges together and make several tightly pleated folds until the wrap is as snug against the fish as you can get it.

3. Press carefully with both hands all around the wrapped fish to force out air.

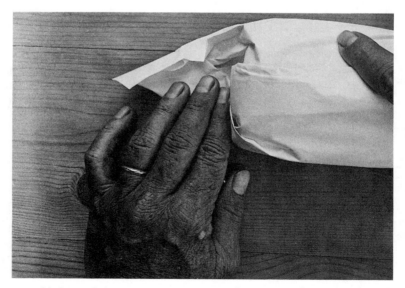

4. Fold the ends in—once more pressing the paper tight against the fish and leaving as little air space as possible.

5. Fold the ends under and secure them to the main wrap with freezer tape.

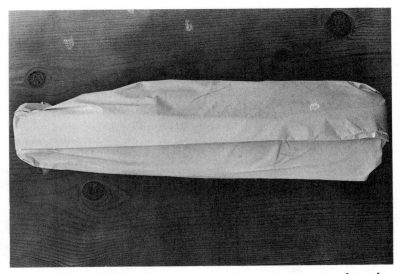

6. Here's the finished package. You may also run freezer tape along the top seam, but if you have pleated the folds snugly enough, this won't be necessary.

THAWING FROZEN FISH

Ideally, wrapped fish should be removed from the freezer a day ahead of time and placed in the refrigerator for slow thawing. It is inadvisable to thaw fish at room temperature, but you can quick-thaw, if need be, by removing the wrap, putting the fish in a plastic bag and immersing it in a pan of cold water.

To thaw fish frozen in a coffee can, I run cold water over the outside of the can until the contents can be slipped out easily when the can is inverted. What comes out is a cylindrical chunk of ice with the fish inside it.

I hold the chunk under running cold water until all visible ice has melted. At this stage, the fish is still solid. I return it to the can, replace the lid, and stand the can upright in a sink of cold water until thawing is complete, draining once or twice as needed. Water need not cover the can. Usually it takes one to two hours to thaw fully.

Do not thaw fish in the can without first melting away the majority of the ice. Otherwise, the fish would be sitting for a considerable time in water, which would sap flavor from the fish and render it mushy.

It really isn't necessary for fish to be fully thawed if you're going to broil, bake or boil it. Cooking time will be increased, of course, but that's of little concern. You could even take a foil-wrapped fish from the freezer and put it directly into the oven for baking, but before doing so be sure to check for punctures. After the fish has cooked for a half hour or so, you can open the foil and add any onion or seasonings you might wish to. Then close the foil and go on with the cooking.

I recommend that fish for frying be thawed completely. It's *possible* to fry partly thawed fish, but inadvisable because the temperature of the oil may drop suddenly below the proper frying level. If the pieces are quite small and you don't have very many to fry, you can get by with it by allowing a minute or two between panfuls to let the grease get properly hot again.

SHIPPING OR TRANSPORTING FISH

Sportsmen often make long trips these days in quest of angling opportunities different from those in their own neighborhoods. There's no longer any good reason why they can't get their catch home—even all the way across the country, or from abroad.

The surest way to bring fish home aboard an airliner is as personal baggage. To prepare it, the first step is to dress the fish and pack it in freezer paper, foil or plastic bags, and have it frozen. Many fishing camps and resorts have freezing facilities on the premises. If not, you can often arrange to have your catch frozen at an ice house or commercial cold storage facility.

Shortly before departure time, the fish can be packed in any kind of sturdy container, preferably—but not necessarily—an insulated chest. In a non-insulated container, excellent insulation can be accomplished simply by surrounding the packed fish with crumpled newspaper. Rip the newspaper sheets apart and wad them loosely by hand. Be sure to arrange a layer of paper on top and bottom of the package, and on all sides.

For maximum results, the package then should be sealed with tape. So packed, you can be confident the fish will come through even an all-day plane trip with flying colors. When you get home, chances are you'll find the fish as solid as when you started.

Similar procedures should be followed if you're shipping your fish, rather than taking it along as baggage; however, it's a good idea to provide additional insulation in case there should be an unforeseen delay in delivery.

If you can get guaranteed same-day delivery, and are certain someone will be on hand to accept the delivery at the appointed time, then the kind of packing described previously will do the job. Otherwise, try this:

Buy one of the inexpensive plastic-foam coolers large enough to hold all your frozen fish. Put the fish inside it, and fill all remaining space with crumpled newspaper. Position the lid tightly and carefully seal all the edges with tape. Run additional strips of tape, for support, around the entire box.

Since such a cooler is flimsy and may not withstand much rough handling, it should be then placed inside a large cardboard box. If the fit between the two boxes isn't snug, once more you use crumpled newspaper for padding.

The resulting package will keep fish frozen for up to three days. I once took delivery of fish which were so packed after they had gone astray and been delayed a full five days. They still were satisfactorily frozen, with only a bit of thawing around the edges.

When you get your fish home, you can transfer them directly to the home freezer, provided they were wrapped properly at the distant location. But if you think a more satisfactory wrapping job can be done at home—for instance, transferring the fish to coffee cans or rewrapping with heavier freezer paper—by all means do so.

Traveling anglers who catch snook can easily bring the frozen fillets home as baggage.

CHAPTER FOUR:

BASIC COOKING METHODS

Many times I've heard the lament, "I just can't cook fish." Maybe you've heard it yourself. Maybe you've *said* it yourself. If so, don't give up yet. Chances are you can pin your failure on just one simple error: overcooking.

Unlike other meats, which often become more tender with longer cooking, fish just gets drier, and usually tougher. Serve up your fish while it's still flaky and juicy and you'll get compliments, not complaints.

No matter whether you're serving plain fried fish or one

of the more elaborate fish recipes with numerous other ingredients, it's important to master the basic cooking methods, and always with the cardinal rule in mind—*don't overcook.*

Fish belongs on the menu regularly. Most of the time it should be prepared by one of the basic methods—frying, broiling, baking or steaming. The delicate fresh-fish flavor, which we have so devoutly strived to maintain in preceding chapters, is thus brought forth in full blossom.

FRYING

Fried fish is the favorite of most folks, calories and cholesterol notwithstanding. Cholesterol can be kept within bounds, of course, by using light vegetable oils for your deep frying and the same oils, or margarine, for your pan-frying (sauteing).

Fried fish should be brown and crisp on the outside, flaky and moist on the inside. And never greasy. All of which is easier said than done. But not really too hard if a few simple procedures and precautions are followed.

First, there's the coating.

If you are frying fish which have been scaled but not skinned—panfish or fillets with the skin left on—the fish should be moistened lightly with water or milk, and dipped in either flour or corn meal or a half-and-half mixture of both.

Because there is no skin to help hold in the juices, skinless fillets or pieces of fish should first be dipped in beaten egg, and then into the coating of choice. My own favorite coating is packaged bread crumbs, which you can buy either seasoned or unseasoned in most markets. The seasoned variety does wonders for mild fish. Packaged corn flake crumbs, cracker meal, corn meal and flour are among other excellent coatings. You might even go for dehydrated mashed potatoes, biscuit mix or pancake mix, each of which had its devotees. Rice flour, which you can find in health food stores, is a bit like corn meal but lighter and does not hold oil. Tasty too! And then, of course, there are numerous prepackaged mixes for coating fish or seafood. You'll have to try them all to determine your own favorites. I use several, but most often reach for seasoned bread crumbs.

Another option is to use a batter instead of breading, which I do from time to time. To make a good basic batter, beat the following ingredients together until fairly smooth (some lumps are fine):

2 eggs
½ tsp. sugar
4 heaping tbsp. flour
Enough milk to obtain consistency of heavy cream

Dip your pieces of fish in the batter. The battering job is easy because you can put the fish and batter in a large bowl, mix thoroughly to coat the fish, and then fork the pieces out of the bowl and directly into the frying pan.

The best way to operate the mechanics of the egg-and-breading method is to start by beating two eggs in a bowl large enough to hold all the fish. Put the fish in the bowl and mix thoroughly to coat the pieces well. With your crumbs in a heavy paper bag, fork the egg-coated pieces of fish into the bag, three or four at a time. Shake the bag, supporting the bottom of it with one hand. Remove the pieces and place them on a platter or sheet of waxed paper. Continue until all pieces are coated, and then proceed with the frying.

In the actual frying, time and temperature are the keys. And if you get the temperature right, the timing will take care of itself.

You not only must get the right temperature, but you must *keep it.* Because of this, fish should be fried in either a cast-iron skillet or one of heavy-gauge aluminum. Thin aluminum pans get too hot, too fast, and then lose heat rapidly when fish are loaded.

The best temperature is in the range of 350 to 375 degrees—400 degrees for very thin fillets that you can almost take out as soon as you pop in. Whole panfish or very thick fillets are best cooked at 350 or so. The majority of fillets run up to a half-inch thick, and 375 is ideal for those. An electric frying pan or deep-cooker with a thermostat can be very helpful. When cooking on the range, use a frying thermometer if at all possible. If you fly by the seat of your pants, you should find a medium-high burner setting about right, but this depends a great deal, of course, on the heat output of the individual burner, and on the amount and depth of the oil. Using the same equipment on the same stove each time, a little trial-and-error should teach you to maintain the proper temperature, even without a thermometer.

If I have any doubts, I test-fry one piece of fish. It should sizzle vigorously as soon as it hits the oil, and brown on one side in not much more than a minute. I like to turn the fish once and brown the other side equally for, at the most, another minute.

In my view, fish for frying should never be cut more than an inch thick, and preferably a half-inch. There should be ample oil in the pan to cover. Don't skimp on the oil. It can be strained afterward and used again. You can even buy electric fryers that filter the oil for you if you do a lot of frying.

My frying implement is a long-handled slotted spoon. Remove the pieces one or two at a dip (if the spoon will hold more than one) and hold over the pan until oil has stopped dripping through the slots in the spoon. Then drop the pieces on absorbent paper.

Stay with it until all the fish is cooked. Don't be pulled away by the phone or doorbell. As soon as the pan is empty —so long as the proper temperature holds—fill it up again, and continue until the job is done. If using a small pan, you may have to add more oil.

You'll notice I haven't mentioned salt and pepper. I sprinkle both over the individual pieces of fish before I dip or coat them. I've tried to take a shortcut by adding salt to the crumbs in the bag, but I never seem to hit it right.

HUSH PUPPIES

Hush puppies go with fried fish like pretzels with beer. They can be prepared beforehand and fried immediately after the fish—at the same temperature and in jig time.

From a meager beginning of corn meal, salt and water, hush puppies have blossomed through the years into many glamorous forms, varied by such additional ingredients as flour, eggs, sugar, shortening, onions, beer, molasses, tomato juice and wine. So adaptable, and so nearly foolproof, is this fried bread that virtually everybody who makes hush puppies regularly has some special ingredient or combination which constitutes "his own special recipe."

If you haven't tried hush puppies before, try this simple style to start. It's the one I still use most of the time, although I do elaborate now and then.

STANDARD HUSH PUPPIES

1 cup self-rising corn meal
1 small onion, grated
Leftover egg from breading fish, if any, or one beaten egg
About ⅓ cup milk

Put the meal in a small bowl and grate the onion directly into it. Add the egg, and then the milk, slowly—stirring until the batter is moist, yet stiff enough to hold shape when formed or when dropped from a spoon. I prefer to form each hush puppy into the shape of a tiny football and drop it into the hot oil by hand. It's faster, however, simply to dip by the half-tablespoon directly into the pan.

Fry at fish-frying temperature, turning once to brown on each side.

Self-rising corn meal is a marvelous convenience. Without it, you would have to mix a bit of flour, baking powder and salt into regular meal. If this becomes necessary, use a ratio of three parts meal to one part flour and add two teaspoons of baking powder and a quarter-teaspoon of salt per cup of mix. Self-rising meal is a stock item throughout the South and in some other sections of the country, but not available everywhere.

As already hinted, it's possible to stray from the basic hush puppy recipe in any number of directions, and I often do. For instance:

1. Chop the onion instead of grating. Or leave the onion out, if you must.

2. Substitute tomato juice, V-8 juice (my favorite), beer or soda pop for the milk.

3. If you like sweet hush puppies (I don't), add a couple teaspoons of molasses, sugar or syrup.

The only thing you really have to guard against in experimenting with your own special hush puppy mixture is getting the batter too soupy. If you use egg, grated onion, molasses or other liquid ingredients, then you naturally have to cut down on the amount of your primary liquid—milk or whatever.

Here is my favorite of all hush puppy recipes—the amount doubled because I usually make it only for company occasions:

HUSH PUPPIES SUPREME

2 cups self-rising meal
1 large onion, grated
1 beaten egg (definitely, whether leftover from fish or not)
Scrambled fish roe (save this up yourself and saute it before-
     hand, or look for small cans of it on grocery shelves).
6 oz. V-8 juice or enough for proper consistency

This recipe will serve seven or eight.

BROILED FISH

It's a snap to turn out delicious broiled fish, but again you should stay close to the scene of action and guard against overcooking. For broiling, choose either fillets or steaks up to an inch thick. These can be broiled without turning. If your steaks are much thicker than an inch, they must be turned, but this is no great problem.

Place the broiler rack about four or five inches (no more) under the heat unit. Allow the unit to preheat for just a few minutes.

Cover a cookie sheet or shallow broiling pan with aluminum foil, turning up the edges all around to minimize cleanup chore later.

Arrange fish on the foil, skin side down if there is a skin side. Sprinkle with salt and black pepper. Place pan under the broiler just long enough to make the surface of the fish fairly hot. Remove the pan and coat all fish generously with butter or margarine. Because the fish is hot, you can spear a large pat of butter with a fork and slide this over each fillet. It's faster, easier, and just as efficient as melting butter

Now return the pan to the oven, leaving the oven door ajar. Allow the fish to broil for about 10 minutes, then remove and check for doneness by sticking a fork gently into the thickest portion. The meat should flake easily all the way through. If so, it's ready. If not, apply another coating of butter and return it to the oven for another three minutes or so.

If you are broiling a steak more than an inch thick, turn it at the end of the ten minutes, brush with butter, and cook for three or four more minutes.

In broiling, fatty fish such as salmon, mackerel and bluefish need be treated no differently from the lean ones, such as bass or snapper. However, you will have to apply the butter more liberally to those varieties which have little fat of their own. And if your diet nixes the use of butter or margarine, choose the fatty kinds of fish, since they broil well enough without it, although much better with it.

SAUTEING

With this type of cooking you use a frying pan with just a little butter, margarine or oil. It is also called "pan broiling" or, particularly if the fish is dusted with flour or other coating, "pan frying."

Somewhat lower temperatures are used than in normal or deep frying, the ideal being about 325 degrees, or medium. Otherwise the surface might brown much too fast, and begin to scorch or burn before the fish is completely cooked. This is especially true when using butter or margarine.

Sauteing can be chosen either for fillets or for small whole fish, such as bluegill or stream trout. If you care about eye-appeal, dust the moistened fish with flour. Unfloured fillets tend to come apart more easily, and unfloured whole fish will end up with numerous breaks in the skin. But if you're going to eat the fish and not take pictures of them, it doesn't matter a bit. And I prefer to leave off the flour, not only because I like the taste of the simple, pan-broiled fish, but also because flouring makes the temperature business even more tricky. Over-browning is too easy with flour.

Sauteed fish should be turned only once, as soon as the first side is browned. And here I should point out that "browned" is a relative term. Without coating, fish does not really take on the overall golden hue provided by batter or crumbs. It should be turned when the edges take on a crisp brownish tone while most of the center portion is an appetizing yellowish-tan. (The color can be much improved by allowing the margarine or butter to turn dark brown in the pan before you start cooking.)

After turning and cooking for another minute or two, test for doneness with a fork, piercing gently to make sure the meat flakes through (or flakes to the bone in the case of whole fish).

After your fish is sauteed, you can add a little lemon juice and soy sauce, scrape the pan with a spatula, and thus make a simple but delicious sauce for pouring over the fish.

POACHING, STEAMING OR BOILING

All three of those terms may be used to describe the same basic cooking procedure, but the word "boiling" as applied to fish raises my hackles a bit. To me, boiling means bubbling around in a lot of water, and with fish this is a real no-no—except when making a fast chowder.

Salmon (and also large trout) are delicious when steaked and poached. So are all the members of the saltwater tuna family. The lean, white-meat fishes of both fresh and salt water are seldom poached, but are not bad at all when prepared this way—especially when served in a salad with some oil or mayonnaise.

Boil barely enough lightly salted water to cover steaks or chunks about one and a half to two inches thick. Add two tablespoons of vegetable oil or margarine to the water. Add fish, cover, and reduce heat to simmer. Simmer for eight or ten minutes, or until fish flakes with a fork. Drain immediately. Most poached fish is served cold.

A common variation—and a considerably better one—is to poach the fish in court bouillon rather than water. Court bouillon is a light broth made by boiling carrots, celery, onion or other vegetables, and spices, along with fish stock. You'll find recipes in Chapter Six.

When you start going over the "fancy" fish recipes in Chapter Six or outside sources, you'll notice that most of them are simply the basic fish-cooking methods we have just outlined—with additions and embellishments, mainly in sauces or additives.

A thorough familiarity with the basic cooking procedures will help assure that any gourmet touches you wish to add through specific recipes turn out the way they're supposed to.

BAKING

A whole baked fish, either with or without the head, is one of the most attractive dishes you can put on the table—and it tastes even better than it looks. Some people just don't like the idea of a fish head on their platter, but there is a practical side as well as a visual one. The head of a fish contains a surprising amount of meat—mostly around the "cheeks" and the top of the head. And in most species, the head meat is even more tasty, and lighter-textured, than the fillet meat. A lot of folks consider it a special treat.

At any rate, choose a fish weighing between two and eight pounds. You can, of course, bake fish weighing a pound or less, but will have to allot at least one fish per person.

Cover a shallow baking pan with aluminum foil, and on this lay the fish, which has been patted dry with a paper towel. The fish can be stuffed or not, as you like. Make sure the oven has been preheated to 350 degrees, and then put the pan on a shelf in the center of the oven.

Although the skin helps retain the juices, you should still do a little basting. As prescribed for broiled fish, you can let the fish heat for a few minutes, and then rub the surface with a pat of butter or margarine. After about 15 or 20 minutes, rub again with butter.

Or, if your dietician isn't looking, you might use bacon. Before putting your fish in the oven, lay two or three strips of bacon across the top. No further basting will be needed, and the skin protects the fish from absorbing more than just a delicate hint of the bacon flavor.

Cooking time will vary from as little as thirty minutes for a two-pound fish to as much as an hour and a half for an eight-pounder. Again, you should rely on testing more than timing, and avoid cooking too long.

With a two- or three-pound fish, test with a fork after 30 or 40 minutes. At the thickest portion, just back of the head, the meat should flake to the bone and not show any pink. If the fish weighs at least five pounds you can safely put off the test until after one hour of cooking.

One reason that testing is important is that thermostats on many older ovens may not be accurate. Whether the fish is put in cold or at room temperature can make a difference too.

Fish weighing less than two pounds will normally bake to perfection in 20 to 30 minutes. Otherwise, they should be treated exactly as larger ones—basting either with butter or bacon strips.

Fillets and steaks can be baked too, but they should either be basted very liberally, or wrapped in aluminum foil to prevent drying. Baking temperature remains 350 degrees. Cooking time probably will be 15 to 30 minutes, depending on the size of the pieces.

This eight-pound redfish is a prime candidate for the baking pan.

CHAPTER FIVE:

COOKING FISH OUTDOORS

Does fish really taste better when you cook it outdoors? Of course it does—but not because any new or different flavors are obtained from the fish itself. Taste, after all (and this is a scientific fact) is far more than the simple result of brushing food against taste buds. Many other elements contribute to it—aroma, texture, color, setting and psychological mood.

Probably you've met people who claim they "don't like fish," yet at a streamside cookout will gobble down theirs—and then snitch your share if you look away for a moment.

Considering the universal enthusiasm for out-of-doors fish cookery, it's strange indeed that so many backyard chefs never give a thought to preparing fish on the home grill. Perhaps they have finally mastered the perfect charcoal steak or hamburger, and are unwilling to risk their neighborhood reputations by trying something new.

It could be, though, that they've tried to grill fish, only to end up with a tough and tasteless product, or have seen fillets flake away before their eyes and disappear through the grill onto the coals.

Grilling fish can indeed be tricky if your barbecuing experience has been limited to red meat. Still, it certainly isn't difficult. The first thing to remember is that ample and frequent basting with butter or a prepared basting sauce is an absolute necessity, even with fatty fish such as salmon and kingfish.

Also, you will find it rather difficult to cook the fish directly on the grill. It can be done, but unless you take great pains in turning, your fish is apt to flake into pieces. Liberal oiling of the grill is helpful, but not infallible.

Some types and cuts of fish handle much better than others when laid on the grill. Fish steaks, for example, are sort of bound by the circling strip of skin. Whole fish, with skin intact, will obviously be more cooperative than a skinless fillet.

Special screens that lie atop your grate represent one way of handling the chore, but the easiest way to solve all such problems is to buy yourself a wire-frame broiler with handle. These are available wherever barbecuing equipment is sold. The fish is held firmly between two wire sides, and can be turned easily. You can baste right through the frame, and there is an added advantage in that all your pieces of fish get turned over in one quick motion.

Before putting a fish into the broiler, it should be rubbed with vegetable oil on both sides. Oil the broiler as well, and for further protection against sticking, you can place strips of bacon between the fish and the wire.

Even if the fish does stick, no tragedy results. You might not be able to put a neat and pretty product on your guests' plates, but when they taste it, they won't mind.

Your grill should be a good four inches above the coals, or six inches for thick steaks or whole small fish. Place the wire broiler on the grill. Turn and baste the fish after a couple of minutes, using melted butter with lemon juice, or a favorite marinade that contains oil. Average-size fillets and small whole fish will require five to ten minutes of cooking on each side. Large ones will take more time, of course. As with all grill cooking, the chef must be observant and ever ready to raise or lower the grill as required by variation in the heat being put forth by the coals. Should the first get too hot—and the grill at its highest point—it may be necessary to sprinkle water on the coals.

You should aim for an attractive browned finish on the outside, with the inside moist and flaky. After a couple of efforts, you'll probably be able to let your eyes be your guide, but until you have built such confidence, test the fish often for doneness. If a fork slides easily all the way through the flesh (to the spine in the case of a whole fish), it's ready. Should you want a double check, use the fork to flake away a bit of meat down to the centermost portion.

Basting should be done at least twice on each side, several times if cooking exceeds ten minutes.

Another fine way to cook fish on your backyard grill is to wrap individual servings in aluminum foil, place the packages on the grill, and turn with tongs from time to time until done—usually 20 to 30 minutes. While you could get exactly the same results in your kitchen oven, your guests will still be delighted because it's served outdoors.

Aluminum-foil cookery is always the same, whatever the setting or the heat source. For more details, see the section on Campfire Cooking later in this chapter.

GRILL-SMOKING

If you own a covered grill or one of the domed barbecue units often called a "kettle cooker" you can produce fish dishes that will make you the rave of the neighborhood. By means of a system called grill-smoking or hot-smoking, your fish will emerge with a marvelous smoke taste, and with much less time and effort than is required for true smoked fish.

Besides the covered grill, you'll need only two important items—a brine solution made by dissolving a cup of salt in three quarts of cold water, and some hickory sawdust or chips. A pound of the chips should be soaked in a half-gallon of water for about a half hour before using.

A low temperature is required for this style of smoke-cooking, the ideal being somewhere in the range of 150 to 300 degrees. With electric or gas grills you have only to set the thermostat. With a charcoal grill, use fewer briquettes than you would for ordinary grilling, and spread them out more thinly in the pan.

Marinate your fish in brine solution for approximately 45 minutes. After your coals are glowing and well spread out, cover them with a heavy handful of the wet sawdust, making sure that every coal is covered.

Now remove fish from the brine and pat dry with a paper towel. Brush with vegetable oil, margarine or butter. Place them on the grill or, better yet, use the wire-frame broiler mentioned previously. Close the cover. The wet sawdust produces plenty of smoke and also helps keep the temperature at the desired low level.

Raise the cover every ten to fifteen minutes to baste the fish liberally and to check the sawdust supply. Add more wet dust as needed. And don't skimp on it.

Cooking time may vary from as little as 30 minutes to, occasionally, a couple of hours—depending not only on the cut and thickness of the fish, but on the temperature of your particular cooker, and variations in temperature caused by the frequent opening or by outside weather influences.

Use the aforementioned checks for doneness. And if your fish seems to be taking extraordinarily long to cook, don't worry about it at all. Nothing can go wrong. You'll just have time to serve another beer or two.

The hot-smoking technique can also be used with a stuffed fish, or with a stuffed double fillet. Marinate the fish first, as described, then fill with the selected dressing and secure the whole shebang in a wire broiler. Then proceed the same way—basting and replacing the sawdust often. Average cooking time for this is about an hour and a half.

SMOKING FISH

Though it may taste much the same, true smoked fish is derived from an entirely different process from grill-smoking. It must be done in a smoking chamber which is made according to rigid requirements of heat and circulation. Of course, smoking is a preservation process. Fish or other meat so treated will last far longer than fresh meats. You can keep smoked fish in your refrigerator (wrapped or covered) for weeks on end. In a freezer, it will last indefinitely.

A workable smoker can be home-made, out of such containers as a large metal garbage can, an old refrigerator, a metal ice chest or a discarded wall oven. All you have to do is arrange wire racks inside, provide for entrance of air at the bottom of the unit plus a small exit hole at the top, and come up with some source of very low heat. In a fireplace or outdoors, a smoldering hardwood fire can provide both heat and smoke for your makeshift smoker. In sheltered areas, an electric hotplate is often used, with a metal pot to hold the wood chips that provide the smoke.

But all that still amounts to a lot of trouble—especially since there are commercially-manufactured smokers that are widely available at very low cost. These work beautifully, take up little storage room in the average household, and need only be plugged in to start working. And one filling of the racks will produce enough smoked fish to last a big family a long time.

You may not be aware of it, but the smoke does not contribute anything to the actual curing of the fish. It only adds flavor. Curing is accomplished by slowly drawing moisture from the flesh.

You begin the moisture-withdrawing process by soaking the fish for quite a long time in a heavy brine solution, after which you remove it from the brine and allow it to air-dry and take on a glaze. Then it is placed in the smoker, on wire racks, and cured for at least several more hours, surrounded within the smoker by smoke and low heat—usually in the neighborhood of 100 to 180 degrees. The heat slowly draws remaining moisture from the fish, and at the same time allows the smoky flavor to penetrate.

Smoking fish at home is a time-consuming process but certainly a simple one. The smoker can be used outside, on a patio or walkway, or in a carport. Or it can be used inside in a fireplace—which is advisable if the outside temperature falls below 70 degrees.

For brine-curing, dissolve two cups of non-iodized salt and two cups of brown sugar in a quart of water. Mix additional amounts in the same proportions if you need more to cover the amount of fish you have.

Fillets make for more satisfactory smoked fish than do steaks, though the latter can be used. Leave the skin on and cut the fillets into pieces small enough to be easily arranged on the racks of your smoker.

Submerge the fish in the brine solution, using a glass, plastic or earthenware bowl as a container. Do not use metal.

Place some sort of weight atop the fish (a dinner plate usually does it) so that no ends stick above the surface. Leave submerged for six hours.

At the end of the brining time, rinse the fish, piece by piece, under cold running water, and lay on paper toweling. Pat all surfaces dry with more towels, and let the fish dry at room temperature for about an hour, or until a noticeable glaze forms on the surface.

As soon as you begin the air-drying period, plug in your

HOMEMADE SMOKER: Garbage can makes a good smoker if rigged with racks inside to hold fish.

smoker for preheating.

The racks of my smoker can be removed in one unit for convenience and portability. When the brined fish takes on its glaze, you arrange the pieces on the racks so they are not touching. Place thicker pieces on the lower racks, since that will be the hottest area during smoking time.

The smoking will take approximately six hours. Smoke is provided by filling a small pan with prepared hickory sawdust and placing it atop the heating unit in the bottom of the smoker. A full pan will burn out in something less than an hour. The manufacturer recommends refilling the pan four times during a six-hour spell of smoking—or about every one and a half hours. But since the smoke has nothing to do with the actual cooking-curing process, you could fill the pan less often or more often, with resulting variations in the amount of "smoky taste." I agree that four pans is about right.

You should begin checking for doneness after four hours. Some of the thin pieces might be ready that soon. If so, the outside will have a dark, rich look to it. But to be doubly sure, take out a piece and break it. The meat should flake easily in the middle.

As you try different species in your smoker, you'll develop your own preferences, but don't be afraid to try any of your favorite kinds. Everything doesn't have to be smoked salmon or smoked sturgeon or smoked sailfish. Smoked fillets of largemouth bass and many other "everyday" fish of fresh and salt water are scrumptious.

I prefer my smoked fish done as simply as possible—just as explained. Some like exotic spices and flavorings, such as onion or garlic, ginger or nutmeg. If you wish to try any or all of these, add them to the brine solution, or rub them into the meat after brining but before smoking.

If you buy one of the commercial home smokers, you'll get detailed instructions not only for fish but for meats and other foods as well.

CAMP STOVE COOKING

A fisherman need not be a camper to enjoy the benefits of a small portable stove. The two-burner models, fueled by LP gas cylinders or by gasoline, can do a good job of frying fish—whether on an overnight campout, an all-day float trip or simply a picnic. For backpacking, or stowing in limited space, you can find a number of small, one-burner units that operate on a variety of fuels. These too can fry fish satisfactorily, provided you use a small pan and don't attempt to cook too many pieces at a time.

One of my own pet uses for a one-burner LP foldable stove is to cook fresh-caught fish for my lunch while I'm out fishing. I cook them right in the skiff if for some reason I don't wish to go ashore.

After all, why should an angler eat a bologna sandwich for his lunch when he can just as easily feast on the very delicacy he's out there to get in the first place?

No great amount of equipment or extra luggage is involved. I carry everything needed in a canvas bag fourteen inches long by ten inches wide by ten inches high—kitchen, pantry, the whole works. Everything but the fish, which is left to angling skill and diligence. Not that I don't have faith in my ability to dredge up enough fish for lunch, but I keep a can of corned beef in that bag too—just in case the frying pan falls overboard or something.

The "shore dinner" is a long-established custom at camps throughout the country and in Canada. The guide carries along the fixings, and when lunch time rolls around, he pulls the boat to shore and cooks the fish while his anglers catch a snooze in the shade.

That's the best approach of all, but without a guide you do it yourself. You can rip through the whole operation in a half hour or less, and maybe still have time for that nap before the next tide, or while waiting for the sun to get just a little lower.

If you can find the right spot on shore, you'll probably

enjoy the whole thing a little more, because you can get out of the boat, and find a nice shady spot and enjoy the stretch and the elbow room. But sometimes the convenient shorelines are too wet, or too thick, or harbor a band of mosquitoes who are looking for a good meal themselves.

In that case—if the water is perfectly calm and your boat very stable—anchor the boat and cook away right there.

Here is a list of supplies I carry in the aforementioned small bag:

EQUIPMENT

1-burner LP stove	Slotted spoon
Plastic forks and spoons	Small pot for boiling water
7-inch iron skillet	2 small plastic bowls
Paper cups (for hot drinks)	Paper towels and plates

SUPPLIES

Small can shortening	Dehydrated onion
Instant coffee	Tea bags
Corn flake crumbs	Salt and pepper
Instant chocolate	Sugar packets
Self-rising corn meal	Artificial sweetener
Instant soups	Dry coffee creamer

It takes almost as much room to list that stuff as to carry it. But none are exceptionally bulky except the stove and the frying pan. Salt, pepper and onion are in shaker-size tubes, which can be tucked inside larger items. The drinks and soup are in small envelopes for individual servings.

A nice by-product of carrying such a kit is that within a couple of minutes you can have a hot drink or cup of soup.

The only thing you *really* need that can't be carried in the kit is a jug of water. Perishables are entirely optional, but can be carried in your ice chest—such things as tomatoes, salad in a plastic bag, or fruit.

I generally carry an egg in the ice chest (inside a small jar) because my favorite coating for skinless fish fillets is beaten egg and corn flake crumbs (see Chapter Four). But when I cook panfish, I just shake them in a bag with corn meal.

At lunch time, I set up the stove and light it and put on the pan with grease so it can heat while other preparations are being made. There is almost no chance of the grease getting too hot on the small stove in open air. In fact, it might not get hot enough if you try to use a thin aluminum skillet instead of cast iron.

While the grease is heating, I clean and fillet the fish, or scale and draw panfish, and sprinkle it with salt and pepper. I beat the egg in one of the plastic bowls if fillets are the course of the day, add the cut-up fillets to the egg, and toss to coat them thoroughly. Then I drop the pieces, two or three at a time, into a paper bag. After a good shake, they are removed to a paper towel.

In the other bowl, I put a teaspoon of dried onion and a little water—letting this sit while I finish mealing the fish. When the onion has sat about five minutes, I add about a cup of self-rising meal and extra water or other handy liquid, if necessary, to make a moist but stiff batter (see hush puppy recipe in Chapter Four).

Now I'm ready to get rolling. If a drop of water makes a loud sizzle in the pan, I start frying the fish by depositing from two to four pieces at a time in the grease. I never crowd too many pieces in the pan, as I must make sure the temperature doesn't fall very much.

I turn the fish once, and as each piece gets golden brown, I remove it with the slotted spoon and deposit it on paper towels.

Once all the fish is cooked, I dip thumb-size bits of the hush puppy batter into the pan, which will easily accommodate about eight or ten puppies at one time. These must be turned once to brown on both sides, and they cook considerably faster than the fish.

When everything is fried, I remove the pan to a safe place to cool, protecting the deck of the boat with paper plates or anything handy that can serve as a hot pad.

I put on a pot of water immediately, and in a few more minutes everyone aboard can have his choice of hot drinks.

After lunch the pan should be cool enough so that I can pour the grease back into its can, wipe the skillet with paper towels, and start putting everything back into the canvas bag. The only other dirty dishes are two bowls and a spoon, which can be rinsed overside and wiped.

There will be some litter, though—plates, cups, plastic forks and copious paper towels, but all is easily crammed into a bag and stowed in a compartment or under a seat for disposal when I get back to shore.

Roughly the same procedures, and the same check-list of supplies, can be used when you're cooking larger quantities of fish on a two-burner stove for more people—perhaps at a picnic, or maybe at streamside for a mealtime rendezvous with other boats. You'll only have to increase the quantities and use larger bowls and pans.

PLANNING A FISH-FRY

Maybe there isn't an easy way to stage a cookout for a large number of people. But at least there's a fairly inexpensive way, if you're a fisherman who manages to stockpile enough fish.

With proper planning, little enough trouble is involved— especially if you can stick your wife (or some of the guests) with taking care of table settings and complementary food items such as beans, salad and cold drinks.

Figure the amount of fish required as follows:

> Fillets—one quarter pound per person
> Steaks—one half pound per person
> Whole fish—one pound per person

Add a couple of pounds "for the pot" if you wish to play it safe, but those figures are surprisingly accurate, and when a rather large and diverse crowd is involved there almost always will be leftovers.

Make most of your preparations at home. Cut the fish into serving-size pieces and salt it. Then pack it in a covered plastic container or a plastic bag for temporary holding in a portable cooler.

Hush puppies also should be mixed in advance and stored in a Tupperware container or a covered bowl. The hush puppy recipe given in Chapter Four will serve five. Make it in necessary multiples, figuring one egg for each two cups of self-rising corn meal.

Your challenge is to turn out quantities of fish, fast enough for all the guests to enjoy while it's piping hot. To do this, you must bring your grease to the appropriate high temperature, keep it there throughout the cooking, and set up an efficient operating system.

As soon as you arrive at the site, fire up the stove. A large bottled-gas deep-fryer, available from many sporting goods stores or mail order catalogs, is by far the most efficient gear for quantity cooking. But you'll have to use it with some frequency in order to justify its cost. Otherwise, a two-burner camp stove can be depended upon to do the job, and to utilize it to best advantage you can consider getting a large, rectangular skillet of cast iron. These are not easily found on housewares counters, but you might get one through a camping equipment specialty store or restaurant supply house, or perhaps a metal shop can turn one out for you at reasonable cost.

If you do decide to have one made, specify dimensions which fit neatly over both burners of your stove. For deep-frying fish on small burners, two fires are better than one.

Without such a special cooker, you must use the largest skillet your main burner will accommodate. The second burner on many camp stoves is an auxiliary and doesn't attain the heat possible with the main one. But you can use a smaller skillet there, and by allowing extra heating time, make helpful use of it.

While the grease heats in your pan (or pans), bread the fish. Beat two or three eggs in a large bowl, fill the bowl with pieces of ready-salted fish, and toss thoroughly. With a fork, bread the pieces by shaking them in a bag with corn flake crumbs, and remove them to a tray or cookie sheet.

Continue until all the fish is breaded. If flies are around, cover the fish with strips of paper towel. Put more paper toweling into one or more large baking pans, or other suitable receptacles, for the fish after it is cooked.

Test-fry one piece of fish to determine if the grease is ready. If you're using two skillets, test a piece in each of them. If the fish browns nicely within two minutes or so, you should be in good shape to start the production line.

Lay out your tray of fish, the hush puppy mix and the take-up pans within easy reach. From now until everything that's uncooked disappears, focus your complete attention on the task at hand.

Drop pieces of fish gently into the pans, until a comfortable capacity is reached. Within a minute, the earliest pieces should be starting to brown. Remove these with a slotted spoon and add others.

Very shortly, you should reach the point where you are constantly dipping up some of the pieces and replacing them. From time to time, hold up on new fish and, instead, drop six or eight hush puppies into the pan with a tablespoon.

At home, I cook all the fish and then all the hush puppies. On a fish-fry, however, I cook ample quantities of both at one time—so that the chow line can begin forming right away.

Rinse your hush puppy spoon in a cup of water now and then. It will make dipping and dropping much easier.

Sooner than you think, the whole job is done. Turn off the burners, join the rest of the picnickers, and enjoy both the hot fish and the compliments you're bound to receive.

CAMPFIRE COOKING

Cooking at an open fire with pots and pans, or wire racks and grills, is not so different from cooking on a camp stove or backyard barbecue. Your main concern will be in creating and maintaining the proper amount of fire or glowing coals to do what you want.

But I do wish to talk about three proven ways to turn out tasty fish with no utensils at all—even though one of these methods requires aluminum foil.

Maybe you'll use one of these recipes someday on a hiking trip, or in an emergency. Or you might decide to build a fire on the spur of the moment when you're out fishing to cook up a little private feast.

Let's start with planked fish, which in some epicurean circles is an elaborate and involved undertaking prepared in the finest kitchens. But in this case, it simply means putting a slab of fish on a plank and propping the plank close to the fire until your meal is done.

All you need is a fish and a flat, or fairly flat, chunk of wood. Dress the fish in double-fillet style (see Chapter Two), and affix the fillet, skin side down, on the plank. The fish must be firmly pinned to the wood, in some manner, all around the edges.

A simple method is to use tacks and a hammer. But if these are not available (and they seldom are, since planking is often a spur-of-the-moment decision), cast around for a substitute.

You could use fish hooks as makeshift tacks. You could wire the fish to the board with stainless leader wire. Failing those, or any other metallic substitute, you could fashion some small wooden pins with your pocket knife, and gouge tiny holes with your knife-point to help seat the pins in the plank.

Getting the fish fastened to the plank is the only hard part. Now you prop the plank upright near your fire. It doesn't much matter whether you have a roaring blaze or a bed of hot coals. Just adjust the distance accordingly, and sit back and relax for a while.

In perhaps 10 or 15 minutes your dinner will be ready. The outside will harden and brown. Test the inside by poking it for flakiness with a pointed stick.

Pull the plank away from the fire and use it for both table and plate. If you have no tableware at all, let the fish cool a little and eat it with your fingers.

The first time I tried planked fish was out of dire necessity, when I camped out overnight involuntarily due to engine failure. I ate, expecting sustenance only—most especially because I had no salt. But, lo and behold, I not only staved off hunger but enjoyed a most delicious repast. However, I do add salt, as well as a bit of butter and lemon, when such luxuries are at hand.

A similar procedure makes use of a flat rock, and is even easier than planking, since the fish doesn't have to be nailed down. Find a rock large enough to accommodate the number of fillets you want to cook. Put the rock smack in the middle of your fire and heat it until it's sizzling hot. Rake it out of the fire with a stick and lay your fish on top of it, skin side down. Don't mind the ashes. They won't get to the meat through the skin.

This system works best with very thin fillets, up to a quarter-inch thick, and they will cook in fifteen minutes or so. When the meat flakes easily away from the skin, dig in.

Cooking with aluminum foil is not necessarily an improvement over the plank and the rock, but it demonstrates progress at work. A lot of anglers, hikers and campers keep some lengths of aluminum foil in their packs or kits—torn from the original roll and folded for tucking away.

A good bed of glowing coals is needed for foil-baking, so start your fire well in advance. Take your choice of either a small fish, around a pound, say, or a couple of fillets.

Place the fish in the center of a piece of foil large enough to allow a good wrap over the top and at both ends. The method of making the wrap is the same as the one illustrated in Chapter Three for freezer wrapping.

However, before wrapping up the dinner package, sprinkle the fish with salt and pepper, and put in either a piece of bacon or a dab of butter, along with a liberal sprinkling of lemon juice.

Now wrap all securely and place directly on the bed of coals. You might rake some coals over the top of the package to hasten cooking, or turn the package frequently with a stick.

If the coals stay glowing hot, twenty minutes should be ample cooking time. Carefully rake the package out of the fire to avoid puncturing the foil. Open it and give the test for doneness. If the meat should still be pink and tough in the middle, refold the package and return it to the fire.

By taking care to handle only the wraps (don't touch the parts that are directly touching the contents), you can handle foil with your fingers almost immediately without risking a bad burn. But don't go blundering to the task. Proceed delicately and use the tips of your fingers only.

If you wish, you can cook an entire meal in one of these foil packages simply by adding some slices of onion, potato and carrots to the fish. Slice all of them quite thin so they will cook as quickly as the fish.

It's True! Cook your fish outdoors and you'll agree that they do taste better.

HOW TO EAT PANFISH (WITHOUT EATING BONES): Many people shun panfish because they fear bones. Here's a simple way to eat them without much worry. You have to use your fingers, but etiquette be hanged at a fish fry!

1. Grasp the dorsal fin near the tail and pull gently upward and outward—moving your grip farther along once or twice, if necessary, to be sure that the small bones which anchor the fins all come out. Discard the fin and bones.

2. Remove the lower (anal) fin in the same manner.

3. Now, by biting to the backbone and sliding the meat off with your teeth, you'll get all the tasty meat. Avoid the rib cage, which is shown intact in the picture, and you'll have no trouble with bones. Note, however, that the meat on the ribs is delicious and a lot of people go to the trouble of picking it away from the bones.

CHAPTER SIX:

RECIPES, SIMPLE AND FANCY

All good cooks have long since discovered that a recipe is no sacred cow which must be held inviolate down to the last pinch of salt and the last flick of a stirring spoon. With fish dishes, you have extra leeway. You can confidently add an ingredient, omit one, or vary quantities. Naturally, you shouldn't dump in two teaspoons of salt for a recipe prescribing a half-teaspoon, but if you prefer a faint hint of onion to a strong jolt, for example, act accordingly.

Nowadays, many recipes are customized for dietary reasons. Obviously, you can (probably should) easily substitute light vegetable oil or margarine whenever butter is called for. Likewise, skim milk can take the place of whole milk, canned milk or cream. Light and/or cholesterol-free mayonnaise is even available these days for baked fish and fish salad recipes.

You can substitute with confidence once you familiarize yourself with the basic cooking methods covered in Chapter Four. Recipes are simply embellishments on the basic methods. The ones that follow include some that require considerable preparation time, and perhaps even a bit of culinary flair. Many others can be prepared easily, taking advantage of numerous shortcuts made possible by today's prepared foods, such as canned soups.

Of course, the best dishes of all are those which, although prepared in a jiffy, make your guests think you have labored all day in the kitchen to create them. We have plenty of those for you, too.

One sharp departure from most cookbooks is the fact that few of these recipes call for a particular kind of fish. Use whatever kinds you like, or have on hand. Again, substitutions are unlimited. A recipe built around a baked red snapper will work just as well for a striped bass or a husky walleye or many other kinds of fish. The list in Chapter Seven makes note of the cooking methods suitable for the various species.

Some of the selected recipes which follow do name a specific fish—out of habit or tradition—but most have been generalized.

APPETIZERS

Fish—other than processed types such as anchovies, fish bits and sardines—are not often seen on the hors d'oeuvres table. Here are a few home preparations which will tastily remedy that oversight.

SEVICHE

1 pound white-meat fish, cut in bite-size pieces
1 large onion, chopped or sliced
1 tomato, chopped fine (remove seeds)
1 small green pepper, chopped fine
2 chili peppers, chopped fine
Tabasco sauce—a few drops
4 to 6 limes or lemons

This is a Latin American favorite, great as an appetizer, a first-course cocktail, or as a snack with cold beer. Is it raw fish? Not at all. Marinading in lime juice cooks it as thoroughly as any fire. Speaking of fire, the chili peppers and Tabasco sauce may be left out if you prefer.

If you plan to serve the seviche as a snack or appetizer the same day, proceed as follows: Put the fish in a crock or glass container. Salt liberally. Add the other ingredients, mix well and then add fresh-squeezed lime juice to cover. Marinate for a few hours, until all pieces are white, with no pinkish centers. As an appetizer, this serves six or eight. Serves fewer when offered as a snack with crackers and drinks.

A slightly different approach is needed if you plan to make seviche and store it in the refrigerator for nibbling over the next few days. Do not include the chopped vegetables and other ingredients in the marinade but simply marinate the salted fish in the lemon juice until it turns white. Use a plastic or glass container with a lid. After marinating, drain the fish, add the chopped vegetables, mix and store.

SMOKED FISH SPREAD

1½ pounds smoked fish
2 tsp. minced onion
2 tsp. celery, chopped fine
1 clove garlic, minced
2 tbsp. sweet pickle relish
1 cup mayonnaise
1 tbsp. mustard
½ tsp. Worcestershire sauce

Flake the fish and stir all ingredients together thoroughly. Chill well before serving on crackers. Makes about 3 cups. To turn this tasty spread into a dip, take a portion of it and thin to desired consistency by slowly stirring in some sour cream.

SMOKED FISH DIP

1 pound smoked fish
1 8-ounce pkg. whipped cream cheese
1 pint sour cream
1 tsp. prepared mustard
3 tbsp. lime juice
3 tbsp. chopped celery
3 tbsp. sweet pickle relish
3 tbsp. finely chopped onion
2 tbsp. mayonnaise

Break up fish well with fork. Mix all ingredients in blender or food processor, Serve with assorted crackers and raw vegetables.

REGAL ROUNDS

1½ cups flaked fish
¼ pound pimento cheese
¼ cup chopped nuts
¼ cup sweet relish
¼ cup crushed pineapple
¾ cup grated coconut

Make two complementing snacks by first mixing the fish with the soft cheese. To half the mixture add chopped nuts; to the other half add relish and pineapple. Form small balls and roll each ball in coconut. Chill.

SEASHELL DELIGHTS

2 cups flaked cooked fish
1 medium onion
1 small green pepper, chopped fine
1 cup celery, chopped fine
1 cup buttered bread crumbs
1 cup mayonnaise
1 tsp. Worcestershire sauce
Parmesan cheese
Salt and pepper

Use seashell (scallop shell) halves, or imitations purchased at kitchen supply shop. Grease well with butter. Mix all ingredients except bread crumbs and cheese. Divide mixture and place on shells. Sprinkle with bread crumbs and Parmesan, and lightly with salt and pepper. Bake at 350 degrees until lightly browned, about 30 minutes. Serves six or seven.

CHOWDERS, SOUPS AND STEWS

From bouillabaisse to catfish stew, fish "soups" are usually hearty main courses which need no accompaniment other than a salad and some bread or crackers. To make any of these dishes, you can start either with boned chunks or fillets, or else with whole dressed fish—stopping to pick out the bones, head and skin after the fish is cooked tender.

NEW ENGLAND CHOWDER

2 pounds fish
Salt pork
3 large potatoes
1 large onion
2 cups milk, cream or half-and-half
Butter, salt and pepper

Start fish simmering in a saucepan with barely enough water to cover. Fry a small piece of salt pork in a skillet. Add diced potatoes and toss. When potatoes are brown, add them, and the sliced onion, to the fish. Simmer a few minutes until potatoes and fish are tender. Add milk or cream, and heat to verge of boiling. Add a large pat of butter. Remove and serve. Individuals should salt and pepper their servings to taste. Serves six.

FAST CHOWDER FOR CAMP OR HOME

1 pound fish
4 medium potatoes
1 small onion
1 can evaporated milk
2 tbsp. butter or margarine
Salt and pepper

Cut potatoes in half and put into saucepan with the sliced onion and the fish. Barely cover with water and boil gently until potatoes are soft when pierced with a fork. Use a large spoon to coarsely mash the fish and potatoes. Stir in a can of evaporated milk and heat to verge of boiling. Add butter. Salt and pepper to taste, individually. Serves four.

FAST FISH STEW

1 pound fish fillet
1 medium onion, chopped
1 one-pound can tomatoes
1 large potato, diced
½ cup water
¼ tsp. salt
1 one-pound can mixed vegetables

Simmer all ingredients except fish and vegetables together for 20 minutes. Add fish and vegetables (including liquid from vegetables) and simmer 15 minutes longer. With long-handled spoon, stir mixture well, breaking fish into small pieces. Serves four.

QUICK MUSHROOM CHOWDER

1 pound fish fillets
¼ pound mushrooms, sliced
4 tbsp. butter
2 cans condensed cream of mushroom soup
1½ cups milk
2 tbsp. chopped pimento
2 tbsp. sherry
Salt and pepper

In a skillet, saute the mushrooms in butter until tender. Add fish and cook about five minutes, breaking fish apart with fork when it is tender. Combine soup with milk and heat separately, stirring until smooth and hot, but not boiling. Add contents of skillet to soup. Stir in pimento and sherry. Add salt and pepper to taste. Serves six.

ONION FISH SOUP SUPREME

1 pound uncooked fish, cut into small pieces
3 slices bacon, diced
6 large onions, sliced
1 stick butter
2 tbsp. Wondra flour
2 chicken bouillon cubes
4 cups boiling water
½ cup grated cheese
Salt and pepper

Fry bacon in a Dutch oven. Add onions, butter and seasonings and cook until onions are soft. Sprinkle with Wondra and stir until smooth. Add boiling water to pan gradually while stirring constantly. Add bouillon cubes and continue to stir until dissolved. Add fish and simmer 10 minutes. Serve in bowls with cheese sprinkled over top. Use any kind of natural cheese you like. Serves six.

EUROPEAN CHOWDER

2 pounds fish
¼ stick butter
1 carrot, diced
1 onion, sliced or chopped
1 tsp. salt
Generous sprinkling of black pepper
1 cup white wine

Melt butter in skillet and brown fish, which need not be cooked through. If you use a Dutch oven, proceed in the same vessel; otherwise, transfer fish to saucepan, add other ingredients, bring to boil and boil gently for 5 minutes— or longer if carrot is not tender. There is no danger of too much boiling, so unless you're pressed for time, simmer another 15 minutes. Add the juice of ½ lemon (optional), stir and serve.

CATFISH STEW, SOUTHERN STYLE

2 slices bacon
1 large onion, chopped
1 large can tomatoes
2 large potatoes, diced
1 tsp. salt
1 cup boiling water
2 tbsp. Worcestershire sauce
¼ cup ketchup
¼ tsp. thyme
1¼ pounds skinned catfish fillets

In Dutch oven or heavy saucepan, fry bacon, remove, drain on paper and crumble back into pan with the chopped onion. Brown onion lightly; then add water, tomatoes and other ingredients except fish. Simmer for 30 minutes, covered. Add fish, cut into bite-size pieces, and simmer 15 more minutes, uncovered. Serves four.

NEW YORK STEW

½ cup celery, diced
1 small onion, chopped
1 carrot, chopped
1 large potato, diced
1½ pounds cod, halibut or other white fish
½ tsp. garlic salt
Flour for thickening
½ cup (small can) shrimp or crab (optional)

Place vegetables in saucepan, barely cover with water, and boil for 15 minutes. Add fish and garlic salt, along with shrimp or crab (if you like), and simmer another 10 minutes. Thicken with flour paste, if necessary. Stir to break up fish and to mix well. Serves four or five.

DELUXE STEW

2 pounds fish
1 onion, sliced
1 cup white wine
1 cup mushrooms, sliced
1 large potato, diced
¼ tsp. thyme
1 small carrot, thinly sliced
½ cup celery, chopped
Generous sprinkling of salt and pepper

Saute fish lightly in a little oil or butter. Add onion slices and brown. Add wine and other ingredients. Cover and simmer about 15 minutes, or until vegetables are tender. Stir lightly to break up fish, and thicken with flour paste, if desired. Serves six.

HASHHOUSE CHOWDER

1 pound fish fillets, cut into bite-size pieces
1 pkg. frozen mixed vegetables
½ stick butter
1 small onion, chopped
½ cup celery, chopped
1¼ cups water
2 cups milk
2 tbsp. tomato sauce
2 tbsp. cornstarch
Salt and pepper

In a large saucepan or, preferably, a Dutch oven, saute the onions and celery in butter, over medium heat, until transparent. Add frozen vegetables, water and fish and simmer until tender, about 15 minutes. Add milk and tomato sauce. Thicken with cornstarch. Salt and pepper to taste. Bring to boiling point and serve immediately. Serves four.

MANHATTAN CHOWDER

1 pound fish
2 slices bacon or equivalent salt pork
1 small onion, chopped
½ green pepper, chopped
1 cup celery, chopped
1 cup fish stock
1 large potato, diced
1 tsp. salt
1 large can tomatoes
½ tsp. pepper

Cut fish into small pieces. Fry bacon until lightly brown, not crisp. Add onion, green pepper and celery. Cook until tender. Add rest of ingredients and simmer for about 20 minutes until potatoes are tender. Serves four.

FRENCH BOUILLABAISSE

2 pounds fish fillets
1 doz. large shrimp, peeled and veined
1 doz. oysters
1 pound lobster meat
6 small scallops
6 clams in shell
½ cup butter
1 large onion, minced
1 garlic clove, minced
2 cups fish stock (made from head and bones)
1 large ripe tomato, peeled
1 tsp. salt
1 lemon, sliced
¼ cup red wine

Saute onion in the butter. Add garlic, fish and other seafood (except clams). A large pan or Dutch oven is needed. Saute about 5 minutes until seafood is cooked. Add stock and other ingredients, and simmer 10 more minutes. Serve by spooning portions of each seafood into bowls, then ladling liquid into each bowl. Float a lemon slice on top. Serves six.

QUICK BOUILLABAISSE

1 fish, about 3 or 4 pounds live weight
½ stick butter
1 onion, minced
1 clove garlic, minced
1 bay leaf
2 cloves
1 tsp. salt
½ tsp. black pepper
1 small can tomatoes
1 can shrimp
1 can clams, in shell

Scale and fillet fish, retaining head, skin and bones. Boil fish parts (except fillets), in enough water to cover, for 20 minutes. Strain. In a large frying pan, saute onion and garlic and then brown fish fillets. Add other ingredients and fish stock, and simmer for 15 minutes.

This dish can be spiced up by adding ¼ cup cooking sherry and a tablespoon of Worcestershire sauce. Serves four.

BAKED FISH RECIPES

As already discussed in Chapter Four, simple baked fish —whether it be a whole dressed fish stuffed or unstuffed, steaks or fillets—requires little more than salt and some butter or other fat for basting. But many attractive variations are available, and they can add not only changes in taste, but in texture and appearance as well.

Several recipes for stuffings will be given first. Each will stuff a three- to six-pound fish. Excess stuffing can be cooked in aluminum foil outside the fish.

RICE-MUSHROOM STUFFING

½ cup butter
1 large onion, minced
2 cups celery, minced
1 cup sliced mushrooms
2½ cups cooked rice
½ tsp. each salt, pepper, sage, thyme

Melt butter, and saute onion, celery and mushrooms about 3 minutes until soft, but not brown. Add other ingredients and mix thoroughly.

BREAD STUFFING

6 tbsp. melted butter
1 small onion, chopped
1 cup celery, chopped
3 cups dry bread crumbs
1 tsp. each: salt, thyme, sage
Dash of pepper

Saute onions and celery in butter until soft, not brown. Put crumbs and seasonings in a bowl and add the sauteed vegetables. Toss thoroughly. If dressing seems too dry, add a couple of tablespoons of water to moisten.

SOUR CREAM STUFFING

¼ cup melted butter
1 small onion, chopped
1 cup celery, chopped
4 cups dry bread cubes
½ cup sour cream
2 tbsp. grated lemon rind
1 tsp. paprika
1 tsp. salt

Cook celery and onion in butter until tender. Combine all ingredients and mix thoroughly.

CORNBREAD STUFFING

3 tbsp. melted butter
1 small onion, chopped
1 cup celery, chopped
1 tbsp. lemon juice
½ tsp. salt
2 cups soft bread crumbs
1 cup cornbread, crumbled

Saute onion and celery in butter until soft. Add other ingredients and toss well but lightly.

BAKED FISH WITH QUICK CLAM STUFFING

1 fish, 3 or 4 pounds, dressed for baking, or two large fillets
Olive oil
¼ cup chopped onion
½ stick butter
1 8-ounce package seasoned stuffing mix
1 6½-ounce can minced clams

In a saucepan, saute onion in butter until clear. Remove pan from burner and add stuffing mix and clams, including liquid from can. Mix well. If stuffing is too dry for your taste, add just a little water. Rub dressed fish with olive oil and place in a foil-lined baking pan. Fill cavity of fish with stuffing. Bake at 350 degrees for about 45 minutes, or until fork pierces easily to bone at thickest part. Extra stuffing can be wrapped in foil and baked alongside. If fillets are used for this recipe, place them in a single layer in greased shallow baking dish. Spoon stuffing on each fillet and press lightly. Bake at 350 degrees for 20 minutes or until fish flakes easily with a fork. Serves six.

FILLETS IN SAVORY SAUCE

1 or 1½ pounds fish fillets
1 tbsp. melted butter
1 pkg. frozen asparagus pieces
2 tbsp. butter
2 tbsp. flour
1 cup milk
1 cup bread crumbs
½ cup American cheese
½ cup processed Swiss cheese
2 tbsp. melted butter
Salt and pepper

Cook the asparagus according to directions on package. Drain. Cut fish into serving-size pieces, place in a greased baking dish, brush with melted butter and sprinkle with salt and pepper. Bake for 10 minutes at 450 degrees. While fish is cooking, melt 2 tbsp. butter in a saucepan. Stir in flour and add dashes of salt and pepper. Add milk all at once, stir and bring to boiling point. Remove from burner and stir in the processed cheeses. After 10 minutes, remove fish from oven and arrange asparagus pieces on top. Pour sauce over. Combine bread crumbs with 2 tbsp. melted butter and sprinkle over the fillets. Return to oven and bake a few minutes longer, until lightly browned. Serves four.

BAKED FILLETS HAWAIIAN

Rice-Mushroom stuffing
1 cup crushed pineapple, well drained
2 large fillets, skinned or skin-on
3 slices bacon (optional)

Mix pineapple with stuffing and spread between fillets. If skin is on the fillets, brush top generously with butter before baking at 350 degrees for 30 to 40 minutes. Test for flakiness with fork. If fillets have no skin, you may wish to place bacon slices across the top to eliminate need for basting. Serves two to four, depending on fillet size.

BAKED FILLETS ALICANTE

1 onion, sliced
1 pound fillets or steaks about 1 inch thick
¼ cup olive oil or vegetable oil
½ cup brown gravy (from mix if necessary)
½ cup white wine
¼ tsp. salt
Sprinkling of pepper
¼ cup nuts, finely chopped

Spread 3 onion slices in bottom of casserole or foil-lined baking dish. Place fish in dish. Mix other ingredients well and pour over fish. Bake at 350 degrees for 20 to 30 minutes. Serves two or three.

POMPANO EN PAPILLOTE
(Also outstanding with sole, or other fine white fish)

1½ cup fish stock
2 whole pompano, 1 pound each, dressed and
    drawn, or 4 fillets
1 tbsp. butter
1 cup crabmeat
1 cup boiled shrimp, chopped
1 large onion, chopped
1 cup sliced mushrooms
1 tbsp. flour
2 egg yolks
¼ cup white wine
Salt and pepper

Use heads to make fish stock by simmering in small amount of water for 30 minutes, then straining. Melt butter in skillet and brown fish at medium heat on both sides. Remove. Saute crab and shrimp lightly, adding more butter if necessary. Add stock, onion and mushrooms and simmer for 5 minutes. Make a paste with the flour and a little stock. Stir in paste, egg yolks, wine, salt and pepper. Using four large squares of parchment paper or aluminum foil, place one whole fish or 2 fillets on each of two squares. Spoon half the sauce over each. Cover each with remaining squares. Fold, seal and bake 20 minutes at 450 degrees. Generously serves two.

FILLETS EN PAPILLOTE

2 pounds fillets
½ cup melted butter
1 tbsp. lemon juice
½ tsp. dill
1 onion, sliced thin
½ pound thin-sliced Swiss cheese
Salt and pepper

Sprinkle fish with salt and pepper. Combine butter, lemon juice, dill and salt. Cut fillets into 6 equal portions. Cut 6 squares of heavy aluminum foil, 12 inches square. Place 1 tsp. of butter mixture on half of each foil square and lay a serving of fish on top of the sauce, then an onion slice, then another tsp. butter mixture and, finally, a slice of cheese. Seal edges of the foil packets and bake at 400 degrees for about 30 minutes. Serves six.

BAKED FILLETS WITH CRAB AND SHRIMP

3 pounds fillets
2 tbsp. butter
2 tbsp. flour
1 cup milk
¼ cup each crabmeat and cooked shrimp, chopped
1 small onion, chopped
¼ cup celery
Salt and pepper

Sprinkle fish with salt and pepper. Melt butter in pan and stir in flour. Slowly add milk. Stir until smooth and thickened. Remove from heat and stir in other ingredients. Roll up filling inside the fillets, securing with toothpicks. Brush outside of fillets with melted butter. Bake at 400 degrees for about 30 minutes, basting twice more. Serves about six.

SANDY'S SEAFOOD SURPRISE

8 or 10 small fish fillets (crappie or other panfish)
1 lb. bay scallops
1 medium onion, chopped
1 large tomato, ripe but firm, chopped
¼ cup celery, chopped
1 bell pepper, chopped
½ lb. fresh mushrooms, sliced
½ lb. grated Swiss cheese
½ lb. grated American cheese
Olive oil
Seasoned salt

Rub fillets with olive oil. Spread fillets, intermingled with scallops, to cover the bottom of a non-stick shallow baking pan. Deep-sea scallops may be substituted for bay scallops, but should be quartered or cut to approximate thickness of the fish. Sprinkle fish and scallops very lightly with seasoned salt. Lightly toss together all chopped vegetables and distribute evenly over the seafood. Mix grated cheeses together and sprinkle over all. Bake at 450 degrees for 10 minutes. Serves six.

This recipe is easily "customized" to your taste. For instance, you can use all fish or all scallops, or add other seafood of similar thickness. And the mix of vegetables can be varied: sliced or chopped carrots, cauliflower, broccoli, etc. Use your favorites (or what you have on hand).

BAKED FILLETS IN WINE

1 pound lean fish fillets
1 cup canned tomatoes, well drained
¼ cup white wine
½ tsp. basil
½ cup shredded Swiss cheese

Place fillets in foil-lined pan and sprinkle with salt and pepper, or with seasoned salt. Spread tomatoes over fillets, slicing tomatoes if whole. Pour wine over fish and sprinkle with basil. Bake at 350 degrees for 15 minutes. Remove and sprinkle with cheese. Bake about five minutes longer, or until fish flakes easily with fork. On serving, spoon juices over each portion. Serves three.

OVEN-FRIED FISH

4-6 panfish or 1 to 2 pounds of steaks or fillets
1 egg, beaten
Prepared bread crumbs or corn flake crumbs
¼ cup butter, melted
1 lemon
Salt and pepper

Salt and pepper the fish to taste, then dip in beaten egg and shake in a bag with the bread crumbs until well coated. Place fish in a foil-lined baking pan (turn edges of foil up all around to form an inner dish). Squeeze lemon into butter. Stir and drizzle over coated fish. Bake at 500 degrees for eight or 10 minutes, until crust is golden and fish tests done with fork. Serves four to six.

FISH ROLLS 'N RICE

1 pound or so fish fillets
3 hard-boiled eggs, chopped
2 tbsp. chopped parsley
2 tbsp. mayonnaise
1 pkg. frozen chopped broccoli, well thawed
2 cups cooked rice
1 can cream of shrimp soup
½ cup white wine.
Salt and pepper

This recipe is best when used with four fillets about six inches long apiece. Sprinkle fish with salt and pepper. Combine eggs, parsley, mayonnaise and mustard. Spoon one fourth of the mixture atop each fillet and roll up. Combine broccoli and rice. In separate bowl, stir together soup and wine until smooth. Stir one cup of the soup-wine mix into rice mixture. Put rice mixture into baking dish and spread evenly. Put fish rolls atop rice. Pour remaining soup-wine mix over fish rolls. Cover with foil and bake at 375 degrees for 20 minutes. Remove foil and bake about 10 minutes more, or until fish flakes with fork. Serves four.

FISH 'N SWISS

1 pound fillets
2 tbsp. chopped parsley
½ cup shredded Swiss cheese
1 tbsp. butter
1 tbsp. flour
¼ tsp. salt
Pepper
½ cup evaporated milk
2 tbsp. sherry

Use four fillets about six inches long apiece. Sprinkle fillets with parsley and salt lightly. Place one fourth of cheese on each fillet and roll up. In a saucepan, melt butter and stir in flour. Sprinkle lightly with salt and pepper and stir again. Add milk and sherry all at once. Stir and cook until mixture is thickened and bubbling. Place fish rolls in a shallow baking dish and pour sauce over. Bake uncovered at 400 degrees for 30 minutes or until fish flakes easily with a fork. If desired, additional cheese can be sprinkled on top and melted by placing in oven for two or three more minutes. Serves four.

FAST FILLETS FLORENTINE

1 pound fillets
1 pkg. frozen whole-leaf spinach
1 pkg. (4 oz.) whipped cream cheese
1 tbsp. butter
4 tsp. flour
1 cube chicken bouillon
1 tbsp. white wine
Salt, pepper, paprika

Cook spinach according to directions. Drain. Spread spinach in a pie plate. Use four fish fillets about six inches long apiece. Season each with salt and pepper and spread one-eighth of the cream cheese on each. Roll up the fillets and place on top of the spinach. In large skillet or saucepan, melt butter and stir in flour. Sprinkle lightly with salt and pepper. Add six ounces of water and the bouillon cube. Heat, stirring constantly, until thick and bubbling. Remove from heat. Gradually stir in remaining cream cheese. Stir in wine. Pour over fillets and sprinkle with paprika. Bake at 350 degrees for 25 minutes. Serves four.

CRABBY FILLETS

2 pounds fish fillets
1 small can chopped mushrooms
1 cup milk
¼ chopped onion
¼ cup butter
1 small can crabmeat
½ cup coarsely crushed saltines
2 tbsp. minced parsley
½ tsp. salt
Pepper
3 tbsp. butter
3 tbsp. flour
¼ white wine
1 cup shredded Swiss cheese
½ tsp. paprika

   Use eight fillets about six inches long each. Drain mushrooms, reserving liquid. Add milk to liquid and set aside. In skillet, saute onion in ¼ cup butter until soft. Add mushrooms, crabmeat, crumbs, parsley, salt and a dash of pepper. Mix and spread over fillets. Fold each fillet over the filling and tuck narrow end underneath. Place fillets, tucked side down, in a baking dish. In saucepan, melt 3 tbsp. butter. Stir in flour and ¼ tsp. salt. Add the milk, liquid from mushrooms and wine. Heat, stirring, until thick and bubbling. Pour over fillets. Bake at 400 degrees for 30 minutes. Sprinkle with cheese and paprika and return to oven for about five minutes longer to brown. Serves eight.

BAKED FISH WITH NEARLY WILD STUFFING

1 4- to 6-pound fish, dressed for baking
1½ cups sliced fresh mushrooms
1 cup shredded carrot
¼ cup chopped onion
¼ cup chopped parsley
¼ cup butter
¼ tsp. salt
1 6-oz. package wild rice/white rice mix
2½ cups water
1 chicken bouillon cube
3 tbsp. melted butter
Pepper

In large saucepan, saute mushrooms, carrots, onion and parsley in ¼ cup butter until tender. Add rice and the seasoning mix from rice package. Stir well. Add water and heat to boiling. Add bouillon and a sprinkle of pepper and stir until cube dissolves. Cover and cook over low heat for 20 minutes. Place fish in a greased baking pan. Brush inside and out with 3 tbsp. of melted butter. Sprinkle inside and out with salt and pepper. Stuff with rice mixture. Wrap extra stuffing in heavy foil and place near fish for about last 30 minutes of baking time. Bake fish at 350 degrees for about 1½ hours, or until fork pierces easily to bone at thickest part. Serves eight.

BAKED FISH WITH REALLY WILD STUFFING

1 3- to 4-pound fish, dressed for baking
4 oz. wild rice
1 cup sliced fresh mushrooms
¼ cup butter
1 cup frozen peas, thawed
¼ cup chopped onion
2 tbsp. chopped pimento
2 tbsp. lemon juice
2 tbsp. melted butter
Salt

Cook wild rice according to instructions on package. Saute mushrooms in ¼-cup butter until tender. Combine rice, mushrooms, peas, onion, pimento and lemon juice. Sprinkle fish with salt. Fill with stuffing and skewer cavity. Brush fish with melted butter. Bake at 350 degrees for one hour or until fork pierces easily to bone at thickest part. Wrap any extra stuffing in foil and bake with fish for last 20 minutes. Brush fish once or twice more with butter during cooking. Serves six.

BAKED FISH MEXICALI

1 four-pound fish (or two or three smaller ones),
     dressed for baking
1 one-pound can tomatoes
½ cup tomato sauce
1 small can Jalapeno peppers, diced
1 onion, sliced thin
Salt and pepper

Sprinkle fish inside and out with salt and pepper and place in a baking dish or casserole. Pour tomatoes and tomato sauce over fish. Scatter diced peppers and sliced onion over all. Cover (aluminum foil is fine) and bake at 425 degrees for 30 minutes to an hour, depending on thickness of fish used. Test after 30 minutes with a fork. Serves four to six.

ZESTY BAKED FISH

1 or 2 fish, 3-4 pounds total, prepared for baking
2 cups Italian seasoned bread crumbs
1 onion, chopped fine
¼ cup sour cream
1 large dill pickle, chopped fine
½ tsp. paprika
Olive oil
Salt and pepper

Sprinkle fish with salt and pepper and place in an oiled baking dish. Combine crumbs, onion, sour cream, pickle and paprika in a bowl. Place stuffing in cavity of fish (or fishes), brush fish with olive oil, cover the pan (foil is fine) and bake at 425 degrees for 30-45 minutes.

BAKED FISH EXOTICA

1 whole fish, dressed—about 6 pounds
¼ cup lime juice
3 cups salted cashew nuts, chopped
¼ pound cheddar cheese, grated
1 small onion, grated
2 bay leaves, crushed
1 cup dry bread crumbs
1 cup milk
½ stick melted butter
¼ cup sherry

Rub fish inside and out with lime juice and sprinkle with salt. Place in foil-lined baking pan. Mix 2½ cups of chopped nuts with the grated cheese, onion, bay leaves and half the bread crumbs. Pour in milk and stir to make a thick paste. Cover fish with paste and sprinkle on the remaining bread crumbs. Bake at 375 degrees for about 45 minutes. In testing for doneness, ease fish up with spatula and test from bottom. Do not break the crust. About three times while fish is baking, dribble mixture of butter and sherry over the top. When done, remove to platter and sprinkle with remaining nuts. Serves four to six.

BAKED FISH, SPANISH STYLE

1 whole dressed fish, about 6 pounds or 3-4 pounds of fillets
1 large onion chopped
¼ cup olive oil
1 No. 2½ can tomatoes
2 tbsp. capers
3-oz. jar stuffed olive bits
1 tsp. salt
½ tsp. black pepper
1 tsp. oregano
2 tsp. chili powder (optional)

Saute onion in olive oil. Add tomatoes and simmer for 5 minutes. Add other ingredients, except fish, and blend. Place fish in foil-lined baking dish. Pour sauce over and bake in 350-degree oven for 30 to 40 minutes. If using whole fish, spoon sauce over fish several times while baking. Serves four to six.

FILLETS WITH SOUR CREAM AND MAYONNAISE

2 pounds fillets
1½ cups sour cream
½ cup mayonnaise
2 scallions, chopped
½ tsp. salt
½ tsp. pepper
4 tbsp. lime juice

Place fillets on foil-lined baking dish. Mix other ingredients together and spread over fish. Bake at 375 degrees for about 30 minutes. Serves three or four.

BAKED FILLETS IN HERB SAUCE

2 pounds fillets
2 tbsp. cornstarch
¼ cup butter or vegetable oil
1 cup bouillon or fish stock
1 tbsp. catsup
½ tsp. mustard
2 tbsp. chopped onion
1 tsp. salt
½ tsp. pepper
½ cup dry bread crumbs

Put fillets into a foil-lined baking dish. Melt butter and blend in cornstarch. Add bouillon slowly, then cook until smooth, stirring constantly. Add other ingredients, except bread crumbs, gradually while stirring. Pour over fish. Toss bread crumbs with a pat of melted butter and sprinkle over fish. Bake at 350 degrees for 30 to 35 minutes. Serves three or four.

FESTIVE BAKED FISH

2 pounds fillets
½ cup French dressing
1½ cups cheese crackers, crushed
2 tbsp. oil

Cut fillets into serving-size pieces. Dip fish in dressing and roll in crumbed crackers. Place on foil-lined pan or cookie sheet. Drizzle oil over fish. Bake quickly in 500-degree oven for 10 to 12 minutes. Test with fork. Serves three or four.

BAKED FISH, FAST BUT FANCY

2 pounds fillets or steaks
Salt and pepper
1 can condensed soup

Place fillets in foil-lined baking pan and sprinkle with salt and pepper. Pour soup (any kind, according to your taste or mood—tomato, mushroom, celery, shrimp, cheddar cheese) into bowl and stir it well. Add a bit of milk to thin it a little if desired, but don't mix in another whole can of liquid as the directions on the can prescribe. Pour soup over fish. Bake in a 400-degree oven about 30 minutes or until tender. If soup doesn't cover fish entirely, baste frequently during cooking. Serve over rice. Serves three or four.

FISH STEAKS WITH A LATIN FLAIR

4 to 6 fish steaks
2 tomatoes, sliced
¼ cup thin-sliced cucumber
¼ cup chopped onion
¼ cup chopped green pepper
1 clove garlic, crushed
¼ stick butter
2 tbsp. lemon juice
Salt and pepper

Place steaks in well-greased or foil-lined baking pan. Arrange slices of tomato and cucumber over steaks. In skillet, saute onion, pepper and garlic in butter until onion is clear. Stir in lemon juice. Sprinkle salt and pepper over fish and pour sauce over. Bake at 375 degrees about 20 minutes, or until fish flakes easily with fork. Serves six.

LUAU BAKED FISH

2-pound fish, dressed for baking
½ cup sliced celery
¼ cup chopped green pepper
¼ cup chopped onion
3 tbsp. butter
1½ cups packaged stuffing mix, herb seasoned
3 tbsp. water
1 tbsp. brown sugar
1 tsp. cornstarch
2 tbsp. water
2 tbsp. lemon juice
2 tbsp. soy sauce
2 tbsp. sliced green onion
1 tbsp. butter
1 clove garlic, minced
Salt and pepper

Cook celery, green pepper and chopped onion in 3 tbsp. butter until tender. Add stuffing mix and 3 tbsp. water. Stir well. Place fish on sheet of greased heavy foil in shallow baking pan or sheet. Sprinkle salt and pepper on fish and in cavity. Fill cavity with stuffing mixture. Seal foil around fish. Bake at 350 degrees for 30 minutes, then open foil and bake for about 15 minutes more, or until fork pierces easily to bone at thickest part. While fish is baking, combine brown sugar and cornstarch in a saucepan. Stir in 2 tbsp. each of water, lemon juice and soy sauce. Add green onion, 1 tbsp. butter and garlic. Cook until thick and bubbly, stirring constantly. Place fish on serving platter and pour sauce over. Serves two or three.

FAST FISH CHOW MEIN

1 pound fish fillets
1 can Chinese vegetables, well drained
½ stick butter
2 tbsp. soy sauce
1 medium onion, sliced

Heat butter in a skillet at medium setting until it turns dark brown. Brown fillets quickly on both sides. Add soy sauce and reduce heat to low. Toss sliced onion with vegetables and arrange over fish. Cover pan and simmer 10 minutes. Serve over rice with Chinese noodles. Serves two or three.

NEAPOLITAN CATFISH

Dressed catfish totaling about 3 pounds
1 large can tomato sauce (15 oz.)
1 tbsp. olive oil
½ tsp. sugar
½ tsp. crushed basil
¼ cup grated Parmesan cheese
Salt, pepper, garlic powder

Place catfish in greased baking pan. Sprinkle with salt, pepper and garlic powder. Cover pan with lid or aluminum foil and bake at 350 degrees for about 45 minutes, or until fish passes fork test. Actual baking time, of course, will depend on size of individual catfish used; six or eight small ones will cook more quickly than three or four larger ones. Near end of baking time, combine in a skillet the tomato sauce, oil, sugar and basil. Simmer about five minutes. When fish is done, drain excess liquid from baking pan and spoon sauce over each fish. Sprinkle fish with Parmesan and bake five minutes longer. Serves six.

ARTIE'S BAKED FISH

2 pounds fish fillets
1 can artichoke hearts, drained
3 cups sliced fresh mushrooms
1 small can tomato sauce
Vegetable oil
Salt, pepper, paprika

Place fillets in foil-lined shallow baking dish. Brush with vegetable oil and sprinkle with salt, pepper and paprika. Bake at 400 degrees for 15 minutes. Cut artichoke hearts in half. Arrange artichokes and mushrooms over fillets and pour tomato sauce over all. Bake for 15 minutes more or until fish flakes easily with fork. Serve over rice. Serves six.

SAUTEED FISH RECIPES

Sauteing, or pan-frying, is suitable for steaks, fillets or small whole panfish. With variation in sauces, and with the many vegetables and fruits that can be sauteed right along with your fish, the possibilities for subtle changes are virtually endless.

A few panfish which are especially good for sauteing with special sauces are crappie, white bass, grunts and small snapper. But many can be used—including, of course, the famous pompano and small trout.

SAUTEED TROUT, RUSSIAN STYLE

6 to 8 small stream trout, dressed
2 eggs, beaten
½ cup milk
1½ cups prepared bread crumbs
Oil for frying
1 stick butter, soft
2 hard-boiled eggs, chopped
2 tbsp. pimento, chopped
Salt and pepper

Salt and pepper trout. Mix beaten eggs and milk; dip trout in mixture, then roll in bread crumbs. Saute in skillet at medium heat, using just a light covering of oil. Make a paste of the butter, hard-boiled eggs and pimento. Spread paste over hot fish and serve immediately. Serves six or eight.

BLACKENED FISH

One of the most widely publicized approaches to fish cooking in recent years has been Blackened Fish, the brainchild of chef Paul Prudhomme of New Orleans, who originally used redfish. Many believe the catchy name "Blackened Redfish" had as much to do with the acceptance of the dish as did its unusual flavoring and cooking treatment. Be that as it may, the dish created a huge demand for redfish in restaurants throughout the country. As a result, overfishing by commercial netters in the Gulf of Mexico became such a threat to the redfish breeding stock that it was finally halted by the federal government. Several states also eliminated or drastically curtailed the commercial sale of inshore redfish, and so Blackened Redfish virtually disappeared from restaurant menus.

To fish-lovers, the loss wasn't all that great. Prudhomme himself declared that fresh tuna was superior to redfish for making Blackened Fish and added that several other species were just as good.

Anglers in the South Atlantic and Gulf states may still enjoy an occasional meal of Blackened Redfish, of course, but they, like Prudhomme, will probably find that several other species are as good, or better. Dolphin is excellent. So is shark, grouper, small black drum and any of the tunas or bonitos. Don't hesitate to try any—if you have enough iced tea or cold beer on hand to make the idea of Blackened Fish sound enjoyable.

And in addition to species variety, we'll also suggest an option in cooking that *may* keep your smoke alarm silent. Packaged blackening mix may be purchased in some seafood markets or gourmet shops. Or mix it yourself, as follows:

BLACKENING MIX

1½ tsp. cayenne pepper
1½ tsp. paprika
3 tsp. salt
1 tsp. onion powder
1 tsp. garlic powder
½ tsp. white pepper
½ tsp black pepper
½ tsp. oregano
½ tsp. thyme
Olive oil
1 stick butter

Mix all dry ingredients thoroughly. Rub three or four single-serving fish fillets with olive oil and dust with blackening mix.

Classically, blackened fish requires a cast iron skillet, which is allowed to get nearly red-hot. At that point, a half-stick of butter is dropped into the pan, followed an instant later by the fillets, which are cooked no more than two minutes a side. Add a bit more butter after turning, if needed. This approach, obviously, will create so much smoke that it's almost imperative to do the cooking outside.

An alternate method will allow you to stay in the kitchen—if barely—while turning out a blackened product that few would be able to tell from the "real" thing. For this, you can use any kind of skillet. A good choice is an aluminum saute pan with a non-stick finish. Put the pan on a burner set at high and add a quarter of a stick of butter. Wait until the butter turns *dark* brown—nearly black—then put in no more than two or three fillets that have been oiled and dusted with blackening mixture. Cook about two minutes on each side, maintaining high heat. If more remains to be cooked, add more butter and allow to turn dark brown once more before proceeding.

SAUTE AMANDINE

Fish fillets, ¼- to ½-inch thick
Flour for dredging
Butter, margarine or oil for cooking
Salt and pepper
¼ cup sliced almonds (more if desired)
Lemon juice

Dredge fish in flour, with salt and pepper. Cover pan with a little oil—up to about ½ inch. Saute fish in oil at medium heat until brown, turning once. Remove. Add sliced almonds and a little butter to same pan, after draining away oil. Stir until almonds are light brown. Pour almonds over fish and sprinkle with lemon.

SPICY SAUTE AMANDINE

2 pounds fillets
1 egg
1 cup milk
Flour
½ cup butter
¼ cup almonds, sliced
2 tbsp. Worcestershire sauce
Juice of 2 lemons
Salt and pepper

Salt and pepper fish. Beat egg and milk together. Dip fish in egg-milk mixture and dredge in flour. In skillet, melt butter and saute fish at medium heat until brown on both sides. Remove fish. Add almonds to skillet and brown. Add lemon juice and Worcestershire sauce. Pour over fish. Serves three or four.

SAUTEED SMOKED FISH WITH EGGS

Smoked fish fillets or small pieces
1 tbsp. butter
Eggs, beaten with salt, pepper and a little milk

If serving-size pieces of smoked fish are used, saute them in butter at medium-low temperature just long enough to heat well, turning once. Remove fish and scramble eggs in the same pan.

If small bits of smoked fish are used, simply mix them with the beaten eggs and scramble all together.

SAUTEED FISH IN SOUR CREAM

2 pounds fillets or steaks
Flour
Salt and pepper
½ tsp. basil, crushed
1 cup sour cream
¼ cup butter or oil
1 onion, sliced

Cut fish into serving-size pieces. Saute onion in butter until tender. Saute fish at medium heat, turning once, until golden brown on both sides. Cover fish with onion, basil and sour cream. Cover and simmer gently for 5 minutes or until fish meets test for doneness. Serves three or four.

SAUTEED FISH WITH VEGETABLES

2 lbs. fish fillets
½ stick butter or margarine
Seasoned salt
¼ cup white wine
1 medium onion, sliced
3 vegetables (at least) from among the following:
    1 stalk celery, chopped
    1 small yellow squash, sliced
    1 small zucchini, sliced
    1 red or green pepper, sliced
    1 ripe but firm tomato cut in small wedges

Sprinkle fillets with seasoned salt. Melt butter or margarine in a large saute pan at medium heat and continue heating until butter covers the bottom of the pan and turns dark brown. Add fish fillets. Turn after about 30 seconds and brown other side for another half-minute. Remove fillets to a nearby platter. Fish need not be done at this point, only browned on both sides. Add onion and vegetables of your choice and cook, stirring frequently, until onion is opaque and other vegetables thoroughly heated. Do not overcook. Sprinkle vegetables lightly with seasoned salt (or salt and black pepper). Add wine. Place fish fillets atop vegetables, cover, reduce heat and simmer for about five minutes. Check fish for doneness. All but the thickest fillets should be cooked. If not, simmer a few minutes more. Serves four or five.

BROILED FISH

In flavor, broiled fish is almost identical to baked fish, and many of the recipes also are similar. The chief difference, of course, is that broiled fish is cooked for shorter periods at high temperatures. Many sauces add zest and variety.

BROILED STEAKS AU GRATIN

4 fish steaks, about ½ inch thick
Butter
1 cup bread crumbs
½ cup cheddar cheese, grated (other kinds may be used)
Salt and pepper

Place steaks in foil-lined baking pan. Brush with melted butter. Sprinkle on bread crumbs and grated cheese until each steak is covered. Broil about 10 minutes. Salt and pepper to taste. Serves four.

SPICY BROILED FISH

2 pounds fillets
½ cup steak sauce
¼ cup ketchup
¼ cup vegetable oil
1 tbsp. vinegar
1 tsp. salt
½ tsp. curry powder

Place fish, skin-side up on foil-lined broiler pan, and spread with sauce made of other six ingredients. Broil about 3 inches from broiler unit for 5 minutes. Turn fish carefully and spread other side with sauce. Broil until fish flakes when tested with fork. Serves four.

BROILED STEAKS BERNAISE

4 fish steaks, about ½ pound each
Salt and pepper
Lemon juice

Bernaise sauce:

2 shallots or green onions, minced
½ cup white wine
½ cup white vinegar
3 egg yolks
¼ cup water
1 cup clarified butter
½ tsp. black pepper
1 tsp. dried tarragon
Lemon juice

Preheat broiler and line a broiler pan with heavy aluminum foil. Salt and pepper the steaks to taste and sprinkle with lemon juice. Set aside. To make the sauce, heat wine and vinegar to boiling in a saucepan. Add shallots and simmer until only one tablespoon remains. Place this with egg yolks, pepper and water in top of a double boiler over simmering water. With a whisk, stir in the butter very gradually. Stir in lemon juice and tarragon. Turn off heat but keep the sauce in the double boiler to stay warm. Broil steaks for about eight minutes on one side and three or four minutes on the other. Test with fork. When fork pierces easily all the way through, the steaks are done. Pour sauce over individual servings.

OVEN BARBECUED STEAKS

4 fish steaks, about ½ pound each
1 cup ketchup
2 tbsp. olive oil
½ tsp. minced garlic
¼ tsp. black pepper
8 drops Tabasco sauce
1 tbsp. Worcestershire sauce
2 tbsp. minced parsley

In a bowl, mix all ingredients well. While sauce is standing, preheat broiler and line a broiling pan with heavy aluminum foil. Place steaks on foil and spread sauce over. Broil for six minutes or so on one side, then turn, spread sauce over other side and broil for three or four more minutes, or until fork pierces through without resistance.

APPLE-CURRY FISH BROCHETTE

1½ pounds thick fish fillets or steaks
¼ cup oil
¼ cup apple juice
2 tbsp. chopped parsley
1 tsp. curry powder
Salt and pepper

Tuna, swordfish or shark is ideal for this recipe, which also can be made on the outdoor grill. Cut fish into one-inch cubes. Sprinkle cubes with salt and pepper. Place in oiled shallow baking dish. Combine and mix remaining ingredients. Pour over fish and let stand for 30 minutes, stirring occasionally. Remove fish and place on skewers. Place skewers on a foil-covered cookie sheet and broil three to four minutes. Turn carefully, brush with remaining mixture and broil three minutes longer. Serve on rice. Serves five or six.

FRUITY FISH FILLETS

2 pounds fish fillets
1 small onion, grated
2 tbsp. lemon juice
2 tbsp. orange juice
2 tsp. grated orange rind
½ tsp. salt
⅛ tsp. grated nutmeg
Black pepper

Arrange fillets in a greased shallow baking dish. Sprinkle with nutmeg and black pepper. Combine other ingredients and pour over fish. Let stand for 15 or 20 minutes. Place under broiler for 15 minutes—possibly longer if fillets are very thick. Baste once or twice during cooking. Serves six.

ZIPPY BROILED FISH

2 pounds fish fillets
1 clove garlic, minced
5 sprigs parsley, chopped
½ stick butter
½ tsp. salt
½ tsp. coarse black pepper

In a small saucepan, melt two tablespoons of butter with the parsley, salt, pepper and minced garlic. Mix well, remove from heat. Brush fish well on both sides with plain butter and broil for 10 minutes in a shallow, foil-lined broiling pan. Turn carefully, spread with more butter and broil five minutes longer. Pour butter-seasoning mixture over and broil another five minutes. Serves five or six.

BROILED FISH STEAKS AU VIN

Fish steaks, about ¾ inch thick
Salt and pepper
Butter
White wine

Place steaks in foil-lined pan and sprinkle with salt and pepper. Place under broiler for a couple of minutes until surface of fish is hot. Remove and brush each piece with a pat of butter held on a fork. Return to broiler and cook two minutes. Remove again, spread more butter and splash liberally with white wine. Return to finish cooking, about 3 minutes. Sprinkle on a little more wine before serving.

QUICK AND SPICY BROILED FILLETS

2 pounds fillets
Salt and pepper
Lime juice
½ cup French dressing

Place fillets in foil-lined baking dish. Sprinkle with salt, pepper and lime juice. Pour on the French dressing. Broil until done—about 5 or 10 minutes, according to thickness. Serves three or four.

NOTE: Either for convenience or added flavor from marinating, this dish can be prepared as instructed and placed in your refrigerator for anywhere from an hour to several hours before cooking. Broiling time will increase slightly.

DEVILED BROILED FILLETS

2 pounds fillets
½ cup chili sauce
2 tbsp. mustard
1 tbsp. Worcestershire sauce
½ tsp. salt
¼ tsp. pepper

Place fillets in foil-lined pan. Mix all other ingredients and spread over fish. Broil for about 5 minutes until done. Serves three or four.

BROILED FISH STEAKS ORIENTAL

2 pounds fish steaks
¼ cup orange juice
¼ cup soy sauce
2 tbsp. ketchup
2 tbsp. oil
1 tbsp. lemon juice
½ tsp. oregano
½ tsp. pepper
1 clove garlic, finely chopped

Place fish in foil-lined baking dish. Combine remaining ingredients and pour over fish; let stand for 30 minutes, turning once. Remove and reserve sauce for basting. Place fish under broiler and broil about 4 to 5 minutes on each side, basting liberally with sauce at least twice on each side. Serves three or four.

POACHED FISH RECIPES

The procedure for poaching fish is given in Chapter Four. The following recipes are for sauces and garnishes that go on after the fish is poached.

Most of the famous poached fish recipes deal with sole or salmon. But substitute any choice fish you have.

Although fish can be poached in salted water, the tastiest results are obtained by poaching them in a court bouillon. This is made at the time of use—never stockpiled in advance.

COURT BOUILLON

3 cups water
1 onion, sliced
¼ cup vinegar
½ tsp. salt
½ tsp. black pepper
1 bay leaf
¼ tsp. thyme

Put all ingredients in pan. Stir. Bring to a boil and simmer at least 30 minutes before cooking fish.

COURT BOUILLON WITH WINE

2 cups water
2 cups white wine
½ tsp. salt
½ tsp. pepper
½ lemon, sliced

Combine all ingredients, bring to a boil, and add fish immediately.

COURT BOUILLON DELUXE

¼ cup each of carrots, celery and onion, chopped
2 tbsp. butter
1 cup red wine
½ tsp. salt
½ tsp. black pepper

Saute the vegetables in the butter until soft, not brown. Add other ingredients and boil 15 minutes before cooking fish.

POACHED FISH HOLLANDAISE

2 pounds fish fillets
Court bouillon
Hollandaise sauce
Lemon slices

Poach fillets in court bouillon, remove to platter and cover with Hollandaise sauce. Garnish with lemon slices. As to the Hollandaise sauce, you're on your own. If I don't feel like making mine from scratch, I use a prepared sauce or a mix. Serves three or four.

POACHED FISH MARNIERE

2 pounds fillet of sole or other mild fish
Court bouillon
1 cup scallions, chopped
½ cup butter
3 tbsp. flour
2 cups milk
½ tsp. salt
½ cup white wine
2 egg yolks, beaten

Poach fish in court bouillon and remove to platter. Saute scallions in butter. Blend in flour and stir constantly while heating, 3 or 4 minutes. Add milk and stir until smooth. Add salt and wine; simmer 5 minutes more. Remove from heat and stir in egg yolks. Spoon sauce over fish. Serves three or four.

POACHED FISH WITH MUSHROOMS

2 pounds fish fillets
Wine-style court bouillon
1 onion, chopped or 2-3 scallions, chopped
Butter
1 small can mushroom slices
1 can condensed cream of mushroom soup

Poach fish in court bouillon and remove to platter. In skillet, brown onion or scallions in a little butter. Add the mushroom slices and soup. Stir until smooth. Add some of the court bouillon—a little at a time—stirring constantly until desired consistency is obtained. Ordinarily, less than a cup of the court bouillon is used. Pour sauce over poached fish. Serves three or four.

POACHED FISH WITH OYSTERS

1½ pounds fish fillets
Court bouillon
1 egg yolk
2 scallions, chopped
Juice of ¼ lemon
12 raw oysters

Poach fish in court bouillon and remove to platter. Cool one cup of the court bouillon and mix in the well-beaten egg yolk, scallions and lemon juices. Simmer for 3 minutes, add oysters, and simmer 3 more minutes. Pour over fish and serve. Serves two or three.

POACHED TROUT NORMANDY

2 large fillets of trout or salmon, up to 2 pounds each
Court bouillon
½ stick butter
1 onion, chopped
¼ cup flour
½ cup white wine
1 pound boiled shrimp, or 1 can shrimp
2 hard-boiled eggs
Salt and pepper to taste

Poach fish in court bouillon and remove to platter, reserving bouillon. Saute the onion in the butter. Blend in the flour. Add one cup of the court bouillon and the wine. Simmer 5 minutes. Chop shrimp and eggs, and stir lightly into sauce. Pour sauce over fish. Serves six.

POACHED FISH SUPREME, WITH WINE

1½ pounds salmon or trout steaks; white-meat fish can
    be used too, and is almost as good
Fish stock or deluxe court bouillon
½ stick butter
2 scallions, chopped
¼ cup flour
½ tsp. each, salt and pepper
1 egg yolk
½ cup white wine
2 cups mashed potatoes, prepared and seasoned

Poach fish in bouillon or stock and remove to platter, reserving liquid. Saute scallions in butter and sprinkle in the flour, blending well. Blend in 2 cups of the fish stock or court bouillon, salt and pepper. Heat until steaming but not boiling. Beat egg yolk and wine together and stir into the hot sauce. Remove from heat. Make a ridge of mashed potatoes all around the fish on the platter. Pour sauce over fish and place under hot broiler until potatoes start to brown. Remove and serve immediately. Serves three or four.

POACHED FISH STEAKS WITH CHEESE SAUCE

Fish steak, or steaks, totaling about 2 pounds
2 cups beer
2 sprigs parsley
1 medium onion, sliced
1 stalk celery, sliced
1 bay leaf
2 whole cloves
4 peppercorns
1 carrot, thinly sliced

Swordfish, salmon and tuna lend themselves especially well to this recipe. Place all ingredients except fish in a large skillet. Bring to boil then turn down heat and simmer for 15 minutes. Add fish steaks. Cover and simmer for 10 minutes. Turn steaks and simmer about five minutes more. Test for flakiness with fork. Serve with following sauce.

SWORDFISH-SALMON CHEESE SAUCE

Broth from preceding recipe
2 tbsp. butter
1 tbsp. flour
½ cup milk
¼ cup Gruyere cheese
¼ cup grated Parmesan cheese
1 egg yolk
2 tbsp. heavy cream
¼ tsp. salt
¼ tsp. pepper

Boil broth until reduced to a half-cup. Strain. In a skillet, melt half the butter, add flour and blend well. Bring milk to a boil in a saucepan and then add slowly to butter-flour mixture, stirring constantly until sauce is smooth. Add the strained broth and cheeses and mix gently. In a separate bowl, beat the egg yolk lightly and add a small amount of the hot sauce. Add to mixture and cook over low heat until sauce thickens. Stir in rest of butter, cream and seasonings. Pour sauce over fish steaks, then place steaks under a hot broiler until lightly browned. Serves four or five.

LEFTOVER OR FLAKED FISH

Leftover fish can be flaked and used in many different ways, but most of the following recipes are so good you may want to poach some fish and make them without waiting for leftovers to turn up.

It makes no difference whether the leftover fish is fried, boiled, broiled, poached or baked. If it's fried, remove as much of the coating as possible before flaking.

FISH RAREBIT

2 cups flaked fish
1 tbsp. butter or margarine
2 tbsp. flour
1 cup milk
½ cup grated cheddar cheese
1 small can mushrooms, drained
1 tsp. chili sauce
2 drops Louisiana hot sauce
Salt

In a saucepan over medium heat, melt butter and blend in flour and a dash of salt. Add milk gradually, stirring and heating until thick. Stir in cheese. When melted, add chili sauce and hot sauce. Stir in flaked fish and mushrooms. Heat and serve over toast or rice. Serves two or three.

FISH AND EGG SCRAMBLE

1 cup flaked fish
1 small onion, chopped
2 tbsp. butter
6 eggs
¼ cup milk
1 tsp. Worcestershire sauce
Salt and pepper

Saute onion in butter over medium heat until transparent. Reduce heat to low. Beat eggs then beat in milk and Worcestershire sauce and pour mixture into skillet with onion. Cook, stirring constantly, until eggs are as firm as you like them. Salt and pepper to taste. Serves three or four.

MacFISH SALAD

2 cups flaked fish
3 cups cooked elbow macaroni
½ cup chopped green pepper
½ cup chopped onion
2 tbsp. wine vinegar
½ cup mayonnaise
1 tsp. spicy mustard
2 hard-boiled eggs, sliced
4 slices bacon, fried crisp

After frying bacon, mix one tablespoon bacon grease with the vinegar, mayonnaise and mustard. If bacon grease clumps, heat the mixture and allow to cool. Mix the other ingredients except eggs and bacon. Stir in the dressing. Arrange sliced eggs over top and sprinkle with crumbled bacon. Serves four.

POTLUCK SEAFOOD SALAD

1 cup flaked fish
1 small can crabmeat
1 small can shrimp
1 cup celery, chopped
¼ cup cucumber, sliced thin
2 tbsp. lemon juice
½ cup mayonnaise
6 strips pimento
Salt and pepper

Toss all ingredients well. Chill and serve on lettuce in small bowls or cocktail cups. Salt and pepper to taste. Add a small strip of pimento to each serving for color. Serves six.

NEPTUNE'S CAESAR SALAD

2 cups flaked fish
1 can green peas
1 cup ripe olives, chopped
1 cup celery, chopped
1 small green pepper, chopped
1 bottle Caesar salad dressing

Toss all ingredients well. Chill thoroughly. Serve on lettuce. Serves six.

SHRIMPY FISH SALAD

1 pound flaked fish
1 cup shrimp, chopped
2 tbsp. lemon juice
½ cup celery, chopped fine
1 tsp. dill weed
½ cup mayonnaise
3 hard boiled eggs, quartered
Salt and pepper

Combine fish and shrimp and toss lightly with lemon juice. Add celery, mayonnaise, onion and dill. Salt and pepper to taste. Chill. Arrange on a bed of lettuce with quartered eggs as garnish, along with several whole shrimp, if available. Serves six.

FRUITY FISH SALAD

2 cups flaked fish
1 apple, chopped
1 banana, sliced
1 8-ounce can pineapple chunks, drained
½ cup raisins
½ cup chopped pecans or walnuts
½ cup mayonnaise
1 tbsp. lemon juice

Combine all ingredients in a two-quart bowl. Toss lightly and serve on lettuce leaves. Serves four.

FISH AND MUSHROOM SALAD

1 cup flaked fish
2 cups sliced fresh mushrooms
1 cup julienne-cut Gruyere cheese
¼ cup chopped parsley
3 tbsp. olive oil
½ tsp. salt
¼ tsp. pepper

Toss all ingredients and serve in individual salad bowls on lettuce or other greens, with blue cheese dressing on the side. Serves four.

TOMATOES STUFFED WITH FISH

1 pound flaked fish
6 medium tomatoes, ripe but firm
1 cup cracker crumbs
1¼ tsp. seasoned salt
½ tsp. dill weed
½ cup celery, chopped
¾ cup mayonnaise
1½ tsp. lemon juice

Cut a slice from the stem end of each tomato and scoop out the pulp and seeds. Drain tomatoes well. Combine all ingredients and fill tomato shells. Chill, then serve on a bed of lettuce. Serves six.

AVOCADO STUFFED WITH FISH

1½ cups cooked fish, flaked
½ cup celery, diced
¼ cup cooked green peas
¼ cup mayonnaise
2 tbsp. sugar
2 tsp. lemon juice
½ tsp. curry powder
½ tsp salt
¼ tsp. pepper
2 ripe avocados, cut in half

Blend mayonnaise, sugar, seasonings and lemon juice. Toss together fish, celery and peas. Blend all lightly and use to stuff four avocado halves.

SHARP FISH SANDWICHES

2 cups flaked fish
½ cup celery, chopped fine
¼ cup onion, chopped fine (optional)
1 cup grated sharp cheddar cheese
6 slices sharp cheddar cheese
¼ cup sweet pickle, chopped fine
½ cup mayonnaise
6 egg rolls

Cut rolls in half, butter and brown lightly under broiler. Combine other ingredients. Divide and spoon the mixture on six halves of rolls. Top each with a slice of cheese. Place under broiler until cheese is barely melted. Serve as is or top with remaining halves of rolls.

FISH AND VEGETABLE MOLD

1½ pounds flaked fish
2 cups water
2 tbsp. lemon juice
1 small onion, chopped
½ tsp. salt
1½ cups cooked rice
½ cup shredded carrot
½ cup thin-sliced celery
¼ cup chopped green pepper
¼ cup sliced green onions
¼ cup raisins
½ cup mayonnaise
2 tsp. soy sauce
1 tsp. sweet relish
½ tsp. ground ginger

In a two-quart bowl, mix fish with rice, carrots, celery, green pepper, green onions and raisins. Mix remaining ingredients well, then toss the two mixtures together. Press into an oiled, one-quart mold or bowl. Chill thoroughly and turn out onto lettuce leaves on a serving platter. Serves four.

SUNNY FISH SANDWICHES

1½ cups flaked fish
1 cup sliced almonds
½ cup chopped celery
½ cup mayonnaise
2 tbsp. lemon juice
12 English muffin halves, toasted and buttered
24 cooked or canned asparagus spears
6 slices American cheese
Paprika

Combine fish, almonds, celery, mayonnaise and lemon juice. Arrange muffin halves on a cookie sheet. Place two asparagus spears on each muffin half. Cover asparagus and muffin with about ⅓ cup of fish mixture. Cut each slice of cheese diagonally into quarters. Place two of cheese triangles on each sandwich. Sprinkle with paprika and bake at 400 degrees for about 15 minutes until cheese melts and sandwiches are well heated. Serves six.

FISH FIESTA CASSEROLE

2 cups flaked cooked fish
1 can cheddar cheese soup
½ cup milk
1 4-oz. can green chilies, chopped and seeded
¼ cup chopped onion
1½ cups broken tortilla chips

Combine soup, milk, chilies and onion in a bowl. Add fish and one cup of chips. Stir lightly and pour into a one-quart casserole (or four ramekins). Top with remaining chips. Bake at 400 degrees for 30 minutes. Serves four.

FISH MOUSSE

1 pound flaked fish
2 tbsp. butter
2 tbsp. cornstarch
¼ cup water
2 eggs, separated
1 cup heavy cream
Salt and pepper

In a saucepan, mix cornstarch with water until smooth. Add butter and place over low heat. Beat in egg yolks. Add salt and pepper. Add fish and mix well. Beat egg whites to the soft-peak stage. Whip cream and fold into the mixture. Fold egg whites into the mixture. Place in an oiled mold and bake in a pan of hot water for 25-30 minutes at 375 degrees. Cool. Chill before serving.

BAKED FISH LOAF

1 chicken bouillon cube
1 cup boiling water
2 cups flaked fish
1½ cups bread cubes
2 eggs, beaten
½ cup celery, chopped
½ cup milk or light cream
1 tsp. onion, grated
1 tsp. salt
2 tsp. lemon juice

Put bouillon cube in water and stir until cube dissolves. Add all other ingredients, mix well, and place in a greased loaf pan. Bake at 350 degrees for about an hour, or until loaf is firm in the center. Serves 6.

ZIPPY FISH LOAF

2 cups flaked fish
1 tbsp. lemon juice
1 cup white sauce (homemade or canned)
½ cup milk
½ tsp. seasoned salt
¼ tsp. pepper
1 egg, beaten
1 cup dry bread crumbs
1 small onion, minced
½ cup celery, chopped

Mix all ingredients well and press into well-greased loaf pan. Bake at 350 degrees until top is brown, about 30 minutes. Serves four.

PARTY PATTIES

2 cups flaked fish
2 eggs, lightly beaten
½ cup ketchup
1 cup crushed saltines
1 small onion, minced

For breading:

1 egg, well beaten
½ cup flour

Patties can be made in advance and held, covered, in refrigerator for several hours or overnight. Stir together first set of ingredients. Shape into balls or patties. Dip each ball into beaten egg and then into flour, coating well. Fry quickly in deep fat at 375 degrees for about one minute or until browned. Serves four.

CREAMED FISH

2 cups flaked fish
½ pound mushrooms, sliced
½ stick butter
2½ cups milk
3 tbsp. cornstarch
½ cup cold water
1 small onion, chopped
Salt and pepper

Saute the onion and mushrooms in the butter over medium heat. Pour in milk and heat barely to boiling. Mix water with cornstarch and add for thickening. Stir in flaked fish. Salt and pepper to taste. Warm well. Serve on toast or rice. Serves four.

FISH NEWBURG

2 egg yolks
1 tbsp. cornstarch
1½ cups milk
2 cups flaked fish
Salt and pepper
Dash of nutmeg
2 tbsp. butter
4 tbsp. sherry

Beat egg yolks with cornstarch until light. Gradually add milk, stirring constantly. Put into top of double boiler (or use a chafing dish) with the fish. Add salt, pepper and nutmeg— all lightly. Cook over briskly boiling water until sauce is quite thick. Add butter and sherry and stir. Serve on rice or toast. Serves five or six.

CHEESY FISH CASSEROLE

1 pound leftover fish, flaked
¼ cup onion
2 tbsp. butter
2 tbsp. flour
¼ tsp. salt
Pepper
1½ cups milk
1 cup shredded American cheese
1 envelope White Sauce mix
1 cup frozen peas, thawed
1 small can mushroom pieces
2 tbsp. butter
1½ cups soft bread crumbs

In a saucepan, cook onion in 2 tbsp. butter until clear. Stir in flour and salt and a sprinkle of pepper. Add one cup of the milk. Cook, stirring, until thick and bubbling. Remove from heat, add cheese and stir until melted. Use remaining half-cup of milk to prepare cream sauce according to instructions on package. Stir cheese mixture, peas and mushrooms into sauce. Stir in flaked fish. Divide into six one-cup individual ramekins. Melt 2 tbsp. butter and toss with bread crumbs. Sprinkle crumbs on casseroles. Bake at 400 degrees for 15 minutes. Serves six.

FISH QUICHE

1 9-inch pie crust
1 cup flaked cooked fish
3 eggs, beaten
1½ cups milk
1 tbsp. flour
1 tsp. Worcestershire sauce
1 tsp. prepared mustard
1 dash Tabasco sauce
½ cup Swiss cheese, shredded
½ cup Gruyere cheese, shredded
¼ tsp. salt

Prepare pie crust and line a nine-inch dish. Line crust with two thicknesses of heavy foil and bake five minutes at 450 degrees. Remove foil and bake five minutes more, or until crust is light brown. Remove crust from oven and reduce heat to 325 degrees. In bowl combine eggs, milk, flour, Worcestershire sauce, mustard, Tabasco and salt. Sprinkle flaked fish over pie crust. Pour mixture over fish and sprinkle with cheeses. Bake at 325 degrees for 45 minutes. NOTE: edges of crust may be covered with foil to prevent overcooking. Allow quiche to cool 15 minutes before serving. Serves six.

FISH AND MUSHROOM PIE

1 cup pastry mix
3 slices bacon
1¼ cups milk, scalded
1 tsp. onion, grated
½ tsp. salt
3 eggs, beaten
2 cups flaked fish
1 can mushrooms, drained (4 oz.)

Prepare pastry mix and line a pie pan. Fry bacon until crisp; drain. To scalded milk add onion and salt. Add the hot milk slowly to beaten eggs, stirring constantly. Spread fish over pie shell. Spread mushrooms over fish. Pour in the milk-egg mixture, and sprinkle crumbled bacon over the top. Bake in 425-degree oven for 20 minutes. Reduce heat to 325 and bake about 15 minutes longer until pie is firm in center. Serves six or eight.

FLAKED FISH SOUFFLE

3 eggs
1 cup milk
2 cups flaked fish
1 cup fish stock
1 small onion, grated
3 tbsp. vinegar
1 tsp. salt
½ tsp. pepper

Separate egg yolks and whip the whites. Beat the egg yolks and stir in the milk. Add everything else except the egg whites and mix well. Fold in the egg whites. Pour into a casserole or glass (Pyrex) bowl. Set in a pan of water and bake at 300 degrees about 45 minutes. Test by inserting a knife in the center. If it comes out clean, fish is done. Serves six.

CREAMY FLAKED FISH CASSEROLE

2 cups flaked fish
½ tsp. salt
2 tbsp. lemon juice
1 tbsp. butter
1 can tomato soup
2 cups mashed potatoes

Mix fish with salt and lemon juice. Add butter to soup and heat, stirring until smooth. Do not boil. Add fish and mix. Pour into shallow casserole or baking dish. Top with mashed potatoes. Place under broiler for a few minutes until potatoes brown. Serves six.

FISH CAKES

3 large potatoes
¼ stick butter
Salt and pepper
1 egg
½ cup evaporated milk
1 cup flaked fish

Boil potatoes; drain and mash thoroughly. Add butter, some salt and pepper, and blend by stirring. Beat egg and milk together and add to potatoes. Beat until light and fluffy. Add the fish and beat again. Form into balls of desired size, or drop from tablespoon, and fry in deep fat at 375 to 400 degrees. Serves six.

CHAPTER SEVEN:

GUIDE TO HOOK-AND-LINE TABLE FISH

This section is designed to answer those famous questions "Is this fish good to eat?" and "How should I cook it?" Once you check the list, and get on the right track, you'll find detailed instructions on cleaning and cooking methods in other chapters.

The following lists provide a quick reference to all the major hook-and-line food fish of North American waters, fresh and salt, with notes concerning their table quality, preferred methods of dressing and preferred methods of cooking.

Various popular and regional names are listed, many of which are merely cross-referenced. In cases where closely related species are involved, the commentary for all is given under a single heading: for instance, the trouts, basses and groupers.

Please note that this listing is in no way intended as a guide to identification of the fish.

No doubt you've seen books or pamphlets which attempt to rate the *taste* of the different species by some such notations as "Excellent" or "Fair." That sort of flat categorization has been deliberately ignored here, because the author feels that any fish worth the bother of cleaning can be made highly enjoyable. The few that should not be bothered with are duly noted.

Several varieties of black bass (this one is a redeye) make delicious eating, but the big specimens are better released.

FRESHWATER FISH

BASS, BLACK. This group includes the largemouth and smallmouth bass, plus several closely-related species such as the spotted or Kentucky bass, redeye bass, Suwannee bass and Guadalupe bass. All can be treated alike. The largemouth is widely regarded as the poorest eating of the lot, but this isn't necessarily so. The largemouth does often have a "muddy" odor and taste, particularly if taken in still, mud-bottomed waters. Since smallmouth and the other species are usually taken in clear or flowing waters, this odd taste is encountered only in a rare very large specimen, and is never pronounced even then. In defense of the largemouth, though, it is unlikely you'll notice any difference between species of similar size caught in similar waters. And, in any event, a largemouth bass which is filleted and skinned loses the objectionable taste.

Bass meat is white, firm and lean. Large specimens are inclined to coarseness—another good reason to release them. Fish of one pound and up should be filleted and skinned. Smaller specimens are delicious when scaled and treated as panfish. They also can be scaled and baked whole, but watch out for that muddy taste if a big largemouth is so treated.

BASS, ROCK. This name is widely used for the striped bass (see below). The common freshwater rock bass is another species entirely, similar to the warmouth and usually prepared as panfish (which see).

BASS, STRIPED. The saltwater striped bass is now a freshwater staple in many different lakes where it has been introduced. It's also called rock bass, rockfish or simply "rock."

The meat is firm and white, suitable for any of the preparation methods you might prefer. The fish can be scaled and filleted, skinned and filleted, or prepared whole.

BASS, WHITE. This is a close relative of the striped bass, and equally good. It can be treated as striped bass, but is usually of panfish size and should be so handled. Larger ones can be scaled and filleted or skinned and filleted.

BASS, YELLOW. Another related species, it is treated as for white bass.

BLUEGILL. See Panfish.

BREAM. See Panfish.

BUFFALO. A sometimes-huge member of the sucker family, buffalo fish are not highly prized, but can be prepared as for carp (which see).

BULLHEAD. See Catfish.

CARP. Small specimens can be quite good and lend themselves to a variety of cooking methods. Carp of any size should be skinned. Large ones are coarse, but good when the meat is boiled and then ground or flaked, and used in chowders or as ground fish for fish cakes and similar uses.

CATFISH. This is a large family and though most are called catfish of one kind or another, you'll hear other names, such as "bullhead" and "pout." Some types, such as the channel catfish and blue catfish, have better table reputations than others, but all are excellent eating.

All catfish should be skinned, and special instructions are given in Chapter Two. Best of all are the little fellows, deep-fried whole. Catfish of between one and six pounds should be filleted after skinning, and the fillets cut into the proper size pieces for frying, or for chowder. Very big catfish can be coarse and sometimes strong. Serving-size pieces cut from big catfish can be fried, but you'll probably like them better in chowders or stews, or baked with sauces.

CHAR. See Trout.

CHUB. Several types of small fish are called chub. Most common is the eastern chub or "fallfish," which averages around eight inches or so, and is good but bony. Scale and dress as for panfish, then score the sides several times with a knife and deep-fry. Scoring helps soften the bones.

CISCO. See Whitefish.

CRAPPIE. See Panfish.

DRUM. Also called sheepshead. This fellow is inclined to coarseness. Small ones are pretty good scaled and baked. Others should be skinned and the meat used for chowder.

EEL. The common eel, although born in the sea, is almost always caught in fresh water and considered a freshwater fish. And a fish it is, despite its snake-like appearance. Clean eels the same way you would catfish (see Chapter Two). They will be easier to handle if you scrub them thoroughly first. Make a cut through the skin all the way around the head. Then peel the skin off with pliers. It will help to nail the head to a board, as with catfish. Smoked and pickled eels are famous delicacies of two continents. You'll like them, too, simply chopped into pieces and fried, baked or stewed.

FALLFISH. See Chub.

GRAYLING. Though not related, the grayling usually is thought of in connection with trout—and the association extends to the dining department. They are handled and prepared similarly to pan-sized trout, although the scales are larger and best scraped off. In taste appeal they are at least equal to trout, and many anglers like them better. They can be pan-fried, poached or broiled.

MUSKELLUNGE. Muskies make fine food. Since even a "small" keeper muskie is big, many are baked—with or without stuffing. Though the scales are small in comparison to the size of the fish, some folks like to scrape them before drawing and preparing, although this is optional. The muskie can also be filleted (and skinned if you prefer), then cut into small pieces for frying or broiling.

PANFISH. We're lumping a lot of different small freshwater fish here—all the sunfish family (called "bream" in the South), plus crappies, perch and the smaller basses. All are excellent food fish and prepared the same way, although you can easily tell a difference in the taste of, say, a crappie and a bluegill.

Instructions for dressing panfish are given in Chapter Two. After cleaning, they are most commonly fried in deep fat, but can just as easily be pan-fried or broiled.

Bluegills, shellcrackers and other sunfish, along with rock bass and warmouth, sometimes develop a "muddy" taste —especially when they reach sizes approaching a pound and are taken from still or murky water. If you do notice such a disagreeable taste in your larger panfish, it can be removed simply by skinning the fish. You can either skin the fish without filleting it, or you can fillet and then skin. Instructions on both methods are found in Chapter Two.

Also, when frying larger panfish whole you may find it advisable to score each side two or three times. This allows the thicker portions to become properly cooked in a short time.

PERCH, SPECKLED. Another name for crappie. See Panfish.

PERCH, WHITE. See Panfish. Also, the white perch is sometimes large enough to prepare whole for baking. It's good all ways.

PERCH, YELLOW. See Panfish.

PICKEREL. Though unbelievably bony, pickerel are delicious, the meat fine and white. In larger members of this family—the pike and muskellunge—the myriad bones are large enough to be picked out. This is almost an impossible job with the pickerel. Try this. Fillet the pickerel, leaving the skin on; lay skin side down on a cutting board, and with a sharp knife slash the meat of each fillet *many times,* close together, from one end of the fillet to the other. Do not cut through the skin (some cuts through the skin can't be avoided and are all right so long as the fillet holds together).

Now cut each fillet into serving-size pieces and deep-fry them. The bones will have been cut even smaller, and further softened by frying. They can be eaten along with the meat.

Pickerel have very small scales which are hard to scrape off. Many people don't bother to do so.

PIKE, NORTHERN. This fish is very bony, as are its relatives, the muskie and pickerel. For specimens up to seven or eight pounds, follow directions given for pickerel. Big ones can be treated as muskie, since the bones are large enough to be picked out—which can be a demanding job, but not impossible and certainly worthwhile.

PIKE, REDFIN. Common in only a few areas, the redfin pike is a little fellow, seldom exceeding a few inches. The scales are so small you can ignore them—and so are those infamous bones of the pike family. Just cut off the head, draw, wash and fry. Delicious.

PUMPKINSEED. See Panfish.

REDBREAST BREAM. See Panfish.

REDEYE. This name is given to certain black bass species—see Bass, Black. Another fish called redeye is a small sunfish—see Panfish.

ROCKFISH or ROCK. See Striped Bass.

SALMON. This group includes the Atlantic salmon of the North Atlantic and its rivers; landlocked salmon and ouananiche salmon, which are strictly freshwater strains of the Atlantic salmon; and any of those same varieties, including the king, and coho, which have been introduced to the Great Lakes.

In their prime, all salmon are famous food fish, and arguments concerning which species are best are mostly opinion. But note that phrase "in their prime." This means fish taken from the sea (or lakes), and stream fish in the early stages of their spawning runs. The longer salmon stay in a stream, the more their flesh deteriorates. But the change in flesh quality is obvious to the eye. Because of this, and because of seasonal knowledge in salmon country, nobody is apt to get stuck with a bad salmon on the table.

Salmon have small scales which are usually ignored, but can be scraped off if you like. The fish then generally is steaked (see instructions in Chapter Two) and the steaks either broiled, baked or poached. Whole salmon of appropriate size may also be baked or poached in a large steaming-vessel. For smoking, salmon should be filleted. Poached salmon may be eaten hot with lemon or a mild sauce, or cold with mayonnaise or another sauce of your choice.

In good salmon-fishing country, there is often a handy cannery where your fish can be canned for a fee or on a share basis.

Landlocked salmon are normally much smaller than the other species and can be treated as for trout. Legal-size salmon of any species which may be too large for the pan, but too small for convenient steaking, can be filleted and prepared as above—broiled or poached.

SAUGER. Often confused with the walleye, the confusion is appropriate when dinner time arrives. The sauger is equally delicious (better, say some), with fine, sweet flesh. Scale and fillet without skinning, then fry or broil. Or you can bake a whole dressed sauger.

SHAD. Most of the raves go to the roe of this fish, but the flesh can also be a gourmet's delight—if you get rid of those bothersome bones. And the simple procedure for doing so is outlined in Chapter Two. In the same chapter, see instructions for turning out a "butterfly" fillet—that is, both fillets cut from the fish but left joined on the underside. If you wish to bake your shad, use the butterfly fillet. Bone each fillet individually, then fold the two fillets back together with stuffing in between. For broiled shad, the fillets can be cut off separately and boned. In any case, scale and behead the shad first. The skin should not be removed.

There are several species of shad in North America. All are good if they are large enough, the larger the better. It isn't much use to fool with a shad under a pound at the very least. The common shad, which is the subject of most angling attention, averages three or four pounds.

SHEEPSHEAD. See Drum.

SHELLCRACKER. See Panfish.

SMELT. Eat these little fellows like peanuts, but enjoy them a lot more. Cut off the heads, draw and scrape. Deep-fry them and eat bones and all if the smelt are tiny ones. If the bones aren't all that tender, eat the meat away from them as with other panfish.

SQUAWFISH. Like the chub of Eastern rivers, the squawfish is an overgrown minnow, and not held in high esteem by anglers. But it is edible. Treat small ones as for panfish. Larger ones can be scaled and filleted. They are best fried.

STEELHEAD. See Trout.

STUMPKNOCKER. See Panfish.

STURGEON. Few anglers are likely ever to see a sturgeon, despite the fact that the great fish occurs in many parts of the country. When a sturgeon is caught in an area where it may be kept (sturgeon are fully protected in some places) it usually is cut into small pieces and smoked, but the flesh is quite good when fried, broiled, baked or used in chowder. A sturgeon can be skinned, then filleted and the fillets cut into usable-size pieces; or the fish can be steaked.

SUCKER. The several species of sucker are relished by many people in various parts of the country. The meat is sweet but bony. Preparing as for pickerel will help. Suckers are generally scaled and filleted, but sometimes have a muddy taste. if so, they should be filleted and skinned. Frying is the rule. Sucker meat is quite good when boiled, the bones picked out, and the flesh used for fish cakes or in recipes calling for flaked fish.

SUNFISH. See Panfish.

TROUT. Almost all cold, unpolluted waters of North American hold trout of one kind or another—natural or introduced, native or hatchery-stocked. All are among the most prized of table fish, but there are definite levels of desirability—reminiscent of graded beef.

To begin with, hatchery fish are lowest on the list. But unless you have a taste mechanism tuned to long years of getting your choice, don't let this bother you, because hatchery trout are delicious. It's just that natives are even more delicious.

Naturally, there are preferences by species, too. And just as naturally, these preferences do vary among individuals. But it's a safe bet that the eastern trout fan will prefer brookies to rainbows or browns, while his western counterpart will take cutthroats or brookies over the same pair of game, but often snubbed, species. But readers who already have their own ideas about the eating of trout won't be swayed by any words printed here, anyway. As for the rest of you, be assured that you'll enjoy any trout that graces your table.

As to handling and preparation, both are covered at length in other chapters. By way of summation, small trout should be slit and drawn, gills removed, and the fish pan fried, poached or baked. They can also be split and broiled. Remove the head if you prefer.

Some trout can get very large in big water. These include not only the sea-run rainbows called steelhead but also landlocked rainbows in large lakes and a few big rivers. Mammoth brown trout are sometimes caught, too. The Dolly Varden grows to huge size as does, of course, the lake trout. If you're lucky enough to get one of those giants and don't prefer to hang it on the wall, it can be treated as for salmon.

WARMOUTH. See Panfish.

WHITEFISH. Great Lakes Whitefish, lake cisco and mountain whitefish are related species which can be treated the same. All are excellent eating. Scale and prepare as for panfish, or scale and fillet, or split. Delicious and well known as smoked fish, whitefish also are good fried, broiled or baked.

SALTWATER FISH

ALBACORE. See Tuna.

AMBERJACK. This fish is very good, a fact which comparatively few anglers realized until recent years. Fillet the fish and skin the fillets as described for extra-large fish in Chapter Two. Then "steak" each of the fillets into serving-size pieces. Trim off any red portions. Prepare any way you like—fried, broiled, chowdered, baked in a sauce of some kind. You may find parasites in the flesh near the tail, but seldom in other areas. Cut out the infested portion and discard. Parasites are common in most species of fish, but noticeable in only a few, so don't let them bother you. They are harmless when the fish is cooked.

ANGELFISH. Angelfish can be skinned and filleted, then fried or used in chowder, but they really don't have much meat and are certainly more valuable when returned to their coral-reef home.

Amberjack, once thought to be "inedible" are now widely regarded as a real treat.

BARRACUDA. Several species of barracuda exist, of which the best known are the Pacific variety and the great barracuda of the South Atlantic and Caribbean. Both of those merit raves on the table, but care must be taken when eating the great barracuda. On occasion they are afflicted with a poison called ciguatera. Unfortunately, there is no way to test whether any particular specimen might be so afflicted; however, the poison seems to be encountered only in larger fish from deep water. Fish of five pounds or less, from the Florida flats or inshore waters, are safe—and delicious. Ciguatera poisoning is rarely fatal, but is painful and lingering—so don't take chances by eating big barracuda.

Pacific barracuda—the species so common off the California coast—is never poisonous. The great barracuda also occurs in the South Pacific, but not in California waters.

Barracudas are easily filleted and skinned and this is by far the best way to prepare them. Any red meat may be trimmed away, although it doesn't seem to impair the taste. Fillets can be cooked in any way you like. They are mild and lean.

BASS, WHITE SEA. This is a potentially much larger Pacific relative of the Atlantic seatrouts and the various Pacific corbinas. The great fish is the favorite of many, and lends itself to just about any type of cleaning or cooking. Fish of appropriate size may be scaled and prepared for baking. They can be filleted and skinned, and with the big ones it's best to do it this way. Few fish are better when fried, but you can cook them any way you prefer. The meat is mild, but flavorful, and white.

BASS, CALIFORNIA BLACK. This huge fish is much like the jewfish or other very large groupers. Generally, it is so big you can only peel the skin off and cut out chunks of meat, butchering them to desired size. Best used in chowders or casseroles, or baked in a sauce, the meat can be fried if cut in thin slices.

BASS, CHANNEL. See Redfish.

BASS, SEA. The common sea bass is also called black bass or blackfish in certain areas of the Atlantic and Gulf Coasts. Most of them are small, but these are one of the sweetest of all panfish. Scale and dress as for other panfish. Occasional ones are large enough to skin and fillet, or even to bake. The meat is fine-grained and white.

BASS, GIANT SEA. See Jewfish; also Bass, California Black.

BASS, KELP. Along with the rock bass and sand bass, which are closely related and often confused, the kelp bass is a good food fish of the California coast. Prepare whole for baking, or fillet and skin for frying or broiling.

BASS, ROCK. See above.

BASS, SAND. See above.

BASS, STRIPED. See same in freshwater listings.

BILLFISH. This catchall term includes marlin, sailfish, spearfish and, sometimes, swordfish. See those listings.

BLACKFISH. See Tautog.

BLUEFISH. Delicious but very rich and oily, the bluefish should be put on ice immediately and eaten as soon as possible after it has left the water. They're best the first day, but can be kept several days if well iced and kept drained. Small "snapper blues" are marvelous panfish, dressed and pan-fried. Larger ones can be filleted "butterfly fashion" as described in Chapter Two, and the fillets stuffed and baked. Or fillets can be cut singly, without scaling or skinning, and broiled. Skinned fillets are good fried. Whole blues of appropriate size can be dressed and baked.

BLUE RUNNER. See Jack.

BLOWFISH. See Puffer.

BONEFISH. Sportsmen hold that bonefish should be released instead of eaten. But if a bonefish is inadvertently killed it can make a fine dinner. The only problem is—you guessed it—bones. Fillet the bonefish butterfly fashion (see Chapter Two). Broil the double fillet, skin side down. When done, a great many bones will "arch up" from the meat. Pick these away carefully and then dig in—but cautiously, because more bones remain in the flesh. The flesh, though, is fat and quite tasty, and needs nothing more than some salt and lemon.

BONITO. See Tuna.

BREAM. Various saltwater panfish are called bream, although no particular one really owns the name. Prepare as for grunts.

BUTTERFISH. This is a generally large panfish, which can be scaled and dressed whole for baking, or scaled and filleted for frying or broiling. Very tasty.

CABEZONE. One of the largest members of the sculpin family, the Pacific cabezone is best when filleted and skinned. Though not much for looks, the fish is quite good eating.

CATFISH. Unlike their freshwater relatives, saltwater catfish are not highly prized as table fare. The common sea catfish is edible but not popular. The gafftopsail catfish is bigger, gamer, and has the reputation of being better to eat as well—having pinkish flesh which is good fried, and great in chowders or stews. Unfortunately, the gafftopsail is covered with a thick slime which makes skinning a distasteful chore. Skin saltwater catfish the same way as freshwater catfish (see Chapter Two).

COBIA. By whatever name it's known, the cobia is an unusual and excellent food fish—unusual because most agree it doesn't taste "like fish." The flavor has been likened to chicken or frog legs. Some other names for the cobia: ling, cabbeo, sergeantfish, crabeater.

Even small cobia have thick, sharklike skin. These should be filleted and then skinned. Large fish can be skinned first, then filleted, and the fillets cut into steaks. Or they can be steaked without filleting. In small pieces, cobia is delicious fried. Large chunks and steaks can be broiled or baked. Meat is dry so use sauce or butter while cooking.

COD. Little need be said about the table qualities of the cod. Most caught these days are smallish and best filleted, either with or without skinning. Butterfly fillets, with skin left on, are the kind you see for salted cod. Salt cod is a staple in many parts of the world, but fresh cod is out of this world. Broil, bake, chowder or cake, you can hardly find a bad way to cook fresh cod.

COD, ROCK. See Rockfish.

COD, TOM. See Tomcod.

CONEY. See Grouper.

CORBINA. This name is applied to various members of the weakfish or sea trout genus of Pacific waters, and also to the California corbina, which is of the same family but more closely resembles the croakers. Regardless, they are all among the best table fish of the Pacific, and prime favorites throughout the tropical Americas. The meat is mild, white, fine-grained. Scale and prepare whole for baking; scale and fillet; fillet and skin. Suit yourself. And cook any way you like. Corbina is the fish usually chosen for making Seviche (see Chapter Six).

CROAKER. Many types of croaker are found along the Atlantic, Pacific and Gulf Coasts. All are very good. Usually pan-size, they should be scaled and dressed whole. Sometimes, however, they reach two pounds or more and can be dressed whole for baking, or filleted. They're excellent fried, baked or broiled.

CUNNER. This is a tasty panfish. Most people like to remove the skin before frying.

DOLPHIN. This deepwater fish occurs around the world and is a choice table variety everywhere. It should be skinned first and then filleted—not vice versa. The fillets are best when baked or broiled, but are also good fried. Keep dolphin well iced, as they grow soft quickly.

DRUM, BLACK. When small—around five pounds or less—black drum are surprisingly good, especially if filleted, skinned and fried. Up to perhaps ten pounds they are good scaled, dressed and baked. Let the giant ones go.

DRUM, RED. See Redfish.

EEL. See listing in Freshwater section.

FLATFISH. Lumped together in this category are all the "doormats"—those strange-looking but invariably excellent tasting fish which are flat and have both eyes on the same, upper, side. Included are the giant halibuts of Atlantic and Pacific, the small dabs, the flounders, flukes and soles. Names are often confused. Several kinds are often represented as "sole" on restaurant menus, and seldom if ever is a customer the wiser.

The rib cavity, encompassing the entrails, is quite small on all flatfish. To clean, simply cut off the head, make a small slit below and remove the entrails. Some cooks prefer to leave the head on, in which case the gills should be removed. Scales on most flatfish are relatively small, though large enough on bigger fish to warrant scaling. Seldom is a flatfish skinned.

Small specimens can be left whole after cleaning, and then can be fried, broiled, baked or pan-fried.

Very large fish—halibut and the occasional huge fluke—can be steaked. Big specimens of any flatfish can be filleted with a long knife, and the fillets cut into suitable pieces for broiling, frying, or for baking with a stuffing.

FLOUNDER. See Flatfish.

FLUKE. See Flatfish.

GREENLING. Two Pacific Coast species share this name. One is the true greenling, a small fish of less than two feet. The other is the lingcod, which is sometimes called greenling because its flesh is green! The lingcod is a great sportfishing favorite and can grow quite large, perhaps as big as a hundred pounds.

Though not closely related, both are popular food fish and should be filleted and skinned, after which they are suitable for all types of preparation. The green flesh of the lingcod is disconcerting but not harmful.

GROUPER. The groupers are a big clan, covering many species from the giant jewfish and Warsaw grouper to tiny coneys. Those of primary interest to anglers—both as prey and as table fare—fall into two main groupings, or genera, as follows.

Genus *Mycteroperca,* represented in the south Atlantic and Gulf by such species as the black, yellowfin, gag and scamp, and in Lower California by such types as the golden and broomtail. Members of this bunch are rather streamlined, as groupers go and, more important for our immediate purposes, somewhat better eating—being finer grained.

Genus *Epinephelus,* represented in the Atlantic by such

groupers as the red, Nassau and the hinds, and in Mexican Pacific waters by the cabrillas. These are less streamlined, more potbellied than the above group and of coarser flesh.

All groupers are usually filleted and skinned, although it's quite all right to draw and prepare them whole for baking. In that case, there is no need to scale, since the tough skin will not be eaten anyway.

Small groupers of any kind provide fillets which are excellent fried. Large groupers of the genus *Mycteroperca* are also quite good for frying if the fillets are sliced rather thin.

All types are great for chowders and stews, while large fillets, or chunks of large fillets, are excellent if baked in a sauce.

GRUNT. These are among the best of saltwater panfish, being preferred by many old-time Floridians to snapper. Scale and prepare them whole for pan-frying. If unusually large, grunts may be scaled and filleted, or even baked whole. There are numerous species, differing in appearance, not taste. However, the largest of all—the white margate grunt, which can reach a weight of seven or eight pounds— tastes very strong when fresh caught, but loses the strong taste after a day or two on ice or a short period of freezing.

HADDOCK. Closely related to the cod, and similar in appearance, haddock may be treated in the same way.

HAKE. Pot-bellied and with a slippery feel, the hake is ignored by many fisherman because of looks. But the meat is white, delicious, almost boneless. Scale and fillet, skin and fillet, or prepare whole for baking.

HALIBUT. See Flatfish.

HOGFISH. Sometimes called hog snapper, though it is not a snapper, the hogfish is thought by many to be the best tasting fish of warm reefs. Certainly, it would be hard to imagine fish flesh any more fine-grained or pure white. Fillet and skin, then fry, broil or boil. When boiled and served with a bit of salt and melted butter, it tastes much like crab or lobster.

HOUNDFISH. This large needlefish is edible and surprisingly good, either filleted or cut in wide steaks. It can be fried or boiled.

JACK. Incredibly, all the jacks have long had the reputation of being very poor table fare—in the States, at least. Actually, they are among the very best of fish, a fact which isn't yet widely known or accepted. They do require a bit of extra cleaning effort, but not much. After being filleted and skinned, the fillets should be cut in half, lengthwise, and the red meat running the length of each piece should be carefully trimmed away—along with some extra bones that lie along that center line. Trimmed fillets may be fried, broiled or boiled for salad. Delicious!

These directions apply to all the jacks, including the jack crevalle, blue runner, bar jack and Almaco or Spanish jack. Perhaps the bar jack is a shade tastier than the others.

JEWFISH: See Grouper.

KINGFISH. See Mackerel; also Whiting.

LADYFISH. Skip this one. The flesh is, of course, edible, but very soft and very bony.

LING. See Cobia; also Hake.

LINGCOD. See Greenling.

LIZARDFISH. Don't let the ugly looks fool you—as they do most fishermen. The lizardfish has beautiful white flesh and a mild flavor—but lots of bones. Scale and prepare as panfish. The odd big ones can be scaled and filleted or filleted and skinned. Score the flesh as advised for pickerel.

LOOKDOWN. Excellent eating and easy to clean. Cut off head and remove entrails, which are in a small pocket just below the gills. Pan-fry or bake the whole fish—or chop in half if you get one too big for your pan. One of the best panfish, the lookdown is similar in flavor to its relative, the pompano.

MACKEREL. Several mackerel species in both the Atlantic and Pacific are similar in table quality. All have oily flesh which is especially well suited to broiling, smoking or salting. Mackerel need not be scaled or skinned. Simply slice off the fillets and broil—or else cut the fillets butterfly-fashion (see Chapter Two) for smoking. Fried mackerel is good, too, and in this case you can skin the fillets. With broiled mackerel, you normally eat the flesh and leave the skin.

Largest of the group is the king mackerel, frequently called kingfish, or king. These generally are steaked, rather than filleted, although small specimens can be treated as regular mackerel. Some of the other mackerel species, particularly the cero of the Atlantic and the sierra of the Pacific, frequently grow large enough to steak.

MARGATE. The white margate of Florida reefs looks exactly like a huge grunt, which indeed it is. See the listing for Grunt. Another species, the black margate, belongs to the same family but is not generally thought of as a grunt because of its large size and dissimilar appearance. The black margate can be scaled and prepared whole for baking, or it can be filleted and skinned for frying or broiling.

MARLIN. These great game fish of the deep oceans should be released. However, when one is brought to dock and escapes the taxidermist, it is usually smoked—and is a real treat. Steaks from marlin are good broiled or baked, but not nearly so good as to influence the deliberate killing of one of these great fish.

MOJARRA. Sometimes called "shad" in South Florida, this is a very good panfish. Scale and prepare whole. Some are large enough to be skinned and filleted.

MOONFISH. See the listing for Lookdown. The moonfish is close to the lookdown in appearance and taste. To make matters more confusing, a lot of people give this name to the lookdown.

MUTTONFISH. See Snapper.

MULLET. The lowly mullet is one of the best-tasting of all fish—very rich and buttery. Eat it soon after catching, or keep it well iced for short periods of time. Because of the oily flesh, poorly-kept mullet become rancid all too quickly. Scale and fillet, then fry or broil. It's also excellent smoked or salted, and the large roe is marvelous. Many mullet are caught by hook-and-line anglers in freshwater rivers, where they are invariably "muddy" tasting. To remove the muddy taste, simply fillet and skin the fish instead of scaling.

PARROT FISH. These grotesque creatures are tricky as table fish—delicious white meat, but the internal organs can be poisonous. Proceed at your own risk, but if you can manage to fillet and skin the fish without cutting into the intestinal area, try boiling the flesh. It tastes like lobster. Also, it can be fried or broiled.

PERCH. This name is incorrectly, but widely, applied to quite a few smallish saltwater fish—especially to the several related types of surf perches or sea perches common everywhere along the Pacific Coast. In the Atlantic, there is the sand perch of southern waters, and some others including the commercially famous "deep sea perch." One true perch of the Atlantic is the white perch, caught in both salt water and in freshwater streams.

There's no need to try separating all these biologically. If a fish wears the name "perch" you can be sure it is an excellent panfish. Scale and prepare whole for pan-frying. Some types do exceed panfish size and can be filleted and skinned or scaled. Usually deep-fried, perch fillets are also good broiled or used in chowder.

PERMIT. When they are small—under seven pounds—it takes a fin-count to distinguish a permit from the common pompano. A cook or gourmet couldn't tell the difference, either. See the listing for Pompano. Large permit—they grow commonly to thirty pounds, and sometimes twice that weight —are also a table treat. However, sportsmen play down their appeal in hopes that most folks will release the big ones. A big permit should be filleted and skinned—not an easy job because the fish is very broad. Next, the fillets should be trimmed of dark meat, then sliced into pieces about the size of minute steaks.

And then comes the surprise. Those pieces of permit will taste like the best veal, but of course are much whiter. You can use them in any veal recipe.

PIGFISH. See Grunt.

PINFISH. More often used for bait than for food, pinfish are good panfish. Scale and prepare for pan-frying.

POLLOCK. Strangely, the pollock is not highly regarded as a food fish by anglers, although it is similar to cod in both appearance and taste. The flesh is not nearly so fine-grained as the cod, and this could be a contributing reason. Still, pollock is quite good when filleted and sliced thin for frying or broiling. And probably nobody could tell the difference from cod when the meat is used in chowders or fish cakes.

POMPANO. According to price, pompano is the best fish in the sea, usually served up in fancy dishes like Amandine and Pompano en Papillote. But there's no need to get fancy. Small pompano, sauteed in a pan, and larger ones baked or broiled can stand on their own as sheer delights—without help from fancy sauces. You needn't scale or skin the fish; simply cut off the head and draw. Fillet, if you prefer. There are several species of pompano, and all are excellent.

PORGY. Here's another panfish favorite which often runs large enough for baking, and is very tasty either way. Bigger ones often are filleted. Whether to scale or to skin is a personal option. Skinning is much easier.

PORKFISH. A vivid black-and-yellow reef fish related to the grunts, it should be handled the same. See the listing for Grunt.

PUFFER. This heading covers the blowfish or swellfish, and also the rabbitfish or silver puffer. Proceed with caution. All are among the very tastiest fish, having a flavor similar to frog legs and, when marketed commercially in the northeastern states, are frequently labeled "sea chicken." However, certain internal organs of some species of puffer can be very poisonous. Apparently there is nothing to fear from the northern variety of blowfish since, as mentioned, huge quantities of them are consumed. Many people in Florida also relish the southern blowfish and rabbitfish, and cases of poisoning are very rare, though usually fatal. Despite the fact that careful cleaning and eviscerating, without rupturing any of the entrails, assures a safe and delicious meal, eating the puffers cannot be recommended here.

RABBITFISH. See Puffer.

RAINBOW RUNNER. A deepwater member of the jack family, this fish is excellent when skinned and trimmed of red meat. Fry or broil.

RAYS. The danger with rays is not in eating them, but in handling. Many have dangerous barbed spikes in the tail. Some can administer an electric shock. Obviously, fishermen don't often bring them home—but the "wings" are very good to eat. A good way to handle rays or skates is to cut off both wings. A layer of cartilage is located in the center of each wing, so you must slice fillets off above and below this cartilage—the same as slicing two fillets away from the backbone of other fishes. Finally, you skin the fillets in the normal manner. Chunks cut from the wings resemble scallops in flavor.

REDFISH. Also called red drum and channel bass, among other names, this is a popular food fish and a very good one in small sizes. Reds up to seven or eight pounds can be filleted and skinned, then fried, broiled, boiled or baked. Up to twelve pounds or so, they are still fine for baking, and for this they should be scaled, drawn and beheaded. Trophy-sized redfish are outrageously coarse, and if eaten at all, should be used in chowder or ground for cakes. Large redfish are now fully protected in many jurisdictions anyway.

ROCKFISH. This name is used for grouper in the Bahamas. See the listing for Grouper. Pacific Coast rockfish species are many, varied—and delicious. Probably more than half the sportsmen's catch in California salt water is made up of rockfish of one species or another. Fillet and skin, and then prepare in any way you prefer.

ROOSTERFISH. Like the jacks, which are close relatives, the roosterfish of Lower California should be filleted and skinned, and trimmed of dark meat. Also like the jack, it's seldom chosen for the table, but quite good.

SAILFISH. Here's another species that is better released. If you *must* bring in a sailfish, by all means smoke it or have it smoked commercially. Its fillets can be broiled or grilled into good fare, but not nearly so good as many other varieties of fish you can catch from the same waters.

SAILOR'S CHOICE. An excellent panfish, this should be scaled and prepared whole for frying.

SALMON. All salmon found in the sea are also found in freshwater streams. Refer to the Freshwater listings for advice on preparing and cooking.

SAWFISH. When it comes to food fish, beauty is as beauty tastes—but the sawfish is so repugnant-looking that nobody realizes it can be steaked (no need to skin) into one of the best dishes you'll ever get out of the sea. Of course, sawfish are rarely caught, even where they're common, so very few people even get a chance to try the broiled steaks.

SCAD. See Jack.

SCAMP. See Grouper.

SCULPIN. This is a large family, its best-known members being the California rockfish (which see).

SCUP. See Porgy.

SEA ROBIN. Not much meat here, but when skinned and filleted it's darn good. Deep-frying is best.

SHAD. Like the salmon, shad are at home in salt water or fresh—ascending rivers to spawn. See the freshwater list for guides to cleaning and cooking.

SEATROUT. Members of this group are also referred to as weakfishes. The Atlantic seatrouts, of which the spotted or speckled trout and the northern or common weakfish are the most prominent, are brothers to the Pacific corbinas and the California white sea bass. Outstanding food fish, they are usually scaled and drawn. Then they can be either filleted or left whole for baking. Along the Gulf coast, the twelve-inchers are frequently dressed whole and served individually, either baked or pan-fried. Usually the head is left on, but this is optional.

SHARK. Most sharks are edible, some highly prized. Steaks cut from the mako shark are as good as swordfish steaks. The common nurse shark of the South is also a good dinner—again, steaked and broiled. The dogfish, a small shark of northern waters, is the original fish in "fish and chips" and still the best, say British fish and chips fanciers—so good that the species has been seriously overfished and substitutes are now the rule. Blacktip, leopard, lemon and other common shark varieties all make good table fare. Because of their tough skin, sharks are difficult to dress, but anglers generally keep only the smaller specimens and these can be handled with patience and good tools. Simply fillet and skin as with softer-skinned fish. All sharks can develop a very disagreeable odor due to uric acid in the flesh, and this turns many fishermen away from trying them. The odor, however, is easily combated. It probably will disappear after the meat has been iced for a few hours, or after it has been frozen for a while. If any lingering odor remains, it can be taken care of by soaking the flesh in lightly salted water for about an hour. Shark meat is firm, white and mild and suitable for any recipe you might care to try.

SHEEPSHEAD. Treat as for porgy.

SHEEPSHEAD, CALIFORNIA. A very delicious fish with flaky white flesh. It should be skinned and filleted. Cook it any way you like, but when boiled and served either hot or cold, it tastes much like lobster.

SKATE. Like rays (which see), skates are very good though shunned by most fishermen. Cut chunks of meat from the "wings," and fry, broil or boil.

SKIPJACK. See Tuna.

SMELT. See listing in Freshwater section.

SNAPPER. The name is commonly given to small bluefish—see that listing. But rightfully the name belongs to a large family of exceptionally fine sport and food fish of the southern Atlantic, southern Pacific and Gulf waters. Best known in the marketplace is the red snapper. Among many others are (Atlantic) the muttonfish, lane, mangrove, schoolmaster, cubera and yellowtail; and (Lower California) striped, colorado, rose, mullet and yellow snappers. The collective Spanish name is "pargo."

While numerous personal preferences are expressed, all snappers, without exception, are marvelous table fish. Small ones, scaled and prepared whole, can be pan-fried or baked as individual servings. Larger ones are most easily filleted and skinned, unless you wish to bake the whole fish, which is a tasty idea. In that case, scale and draw it and cut off the head. Bake it stuffed or unstuffed. Even the hugest snappers, such as the cubera, are delicious and tender. Skin the giants and cut the meat into slices or large chunks for baking.

SNOOK. This is one of the best southern fish. It yields very thick fillets and should always be filleted and skinned. Without skinning, it has a soapy taste. Slice the fillets into small pieces, or "fingers," and deep-fry. It's also good broiled or baked, or used in chowder.

SOLE. See Flatfish.

SPADEFISH. Similar to angelfish but better as food. Fillet and skin, then fry or broil.

SPOT. A highly popular panfish. Scale, dress and fry.

SQUIRRELFISH. A good panfish, but difficult to clean and handle, because of wicked gill covers and spines. Since you're bound to catch other good panfish in the same waters, pass it up.

SWORDFISH. The steaks are justly famous, but its popularity as a food fish has caused stocks to diminish to a critical level. Sportsmen are no longer very likely to bring in a swordfish, but any who does can fillet the fish—a big job— and cut steaks from the fillets. Suitable for any number of preparations, swordfish steaks are at their best when grilled or broiled and served with your choice of mild sauces.

TARPON. The meat is dark and mushy. This fish is never eaten in the States, though in some places it's dried or made into fish cakes.

TALLY, OCEAN. See Triggerfish.

TAUTOG. Also called blackfish, this is a delicious fish which should be filleted and skinned. The white meat then can be fried, boiled or broiled.

TOMCOD. Though not as highly regarded as its larger relative, the cod, the tomcod is just about as good on the table, and can be treated the same way.

TORO. A good panfish. Scale, dress and pan-fry. Or fillet and skin if you have enough of the larger specimens.

TRIGGERFISH. The several varieties of triggerfish, including the beautiful queen trigger and the large ocean tally (sometimes called turbot), are very good and preferred by some over snapper. But they are tough to clean because of the very leathery skin. They can be skinned first, then filleted, or else filleted and then skinned. Either way, take care. You can easily break a thin stainless-steel knife trying to dress a large triggerfish. Worse still, the blade might slip on the rough skin and give you a nasty cut. The fillets can be fried or broiled.

TRIPLETAIL. Odd-looking but fine eating, the tripletail is best filleted and skinned. It can be fried, broiled or baked.

TROUT. See Seatrout. Some of the true freshwater trout do run to sea and can be caught along the coast in certain northern areas. See Trout in the Freshwater list.

TUNA. Americans, whether they catch their tuna or buy them in cans, almost invariably express their preferences in terms of the lightest, prettiest meat. Thus the "finest" tuna is the white-meat albacore of the Pacific, and the "worst" are the dark-meat bonitos. Yellowfin, blackfin and small bluefin tuna are happily accepted as "light" compromises. Actually, the dark tuna are said to be the most nutritious and are the preferred species in some parts of the world.

Regardless of all that, any tuna can be boiled and made into a good salad. Fillet, skin and cut it into pieces of desired size. Pieces of most tunas—especially the yellowfin and blackfin, but also the dark-meated types—can be sauteed or broiled with butter, and taste more like baby beef than fish. And in case you haven't tasted baby beef, it's mild and enjoyable but not as full-flavored as mature beef. Yellowfin tuna steaks are served in many restaurants, usually to much praise from the customers. Raw slivers of tuna are, of course, among the most coveted of fish flesh by lovers of sushi and sashimi.

TURBOT. See the listing for Triggerfish. The name also is used for some flounders; see Flatfish.

WAHOO. An excellent offshore game and food fish, similar in appearance and taste to the king mackerel. Best when steaked and broiled, it is also a great fish for smoking.

WHITING. These are small, slender fish of croaker-like appearance. They're most often scaled, drawn and beheaded, then pan-fried. The flesh is soft. Whiting should be used immediately after catching. They're also called "kingfish" or "king whiting."

WRASSE. The commonly-caught wrasses are the hogfish, tautog and California sheepshead. See those headings. Most other members of this family are also delicious, with very white and mild flesh.

YELLOWTAIL, ATLANTIC. See Snapper.

YELLOWTAIL, PACIFIC. A California favorite, yellowtail can be either filleted and skinned, or steaked. They're delicious fried, broiled—or just about any way you care to prepare them.

CHAPTER 8:

CALORIE LISTING

All of the following calorie counts are based on 3½-oz. portions of edible food.

Perch, white 118
Perch, yellow 91
Pollock 128
Porgy and Scup 112
Redfish (channel bass) 122
Redhorse, silver 98
Sanddab (see Flatfish)
Seabass 96
Seatrout, spotted 105
Shad, baked 201
Sheepshead, Atlantic 113
Skate or ray 98
Smelt 98
Snapper, red, gray, yellowtail 93
Snook 95
Sole (see Flatfish)
Sturgeon, steamed 160
Suckers, including white 104
Sucker, carp 111
Swordfish, broiled 174
Tautog 89
Tilefish, baked 138
Trout, brook 101
Tuna, bluefin 145
Tuna, yellowfin 133
Tuna salad 170
Whitefish, baked, stuffed 215
Whiting 105
Wreckfish 114
Yellowtail, Pacific 138

INDEX

Additional photo credits: Skinning catfish—Lefty Kreh; Boning Shad—Howard Brant.

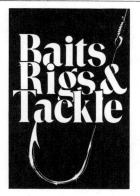

More Where This Came From...

A perfect companion to From Hook to Table is author Vic Dunaway's *Complete Book of Baits, Rigs and Tackle,* the fishing world's all-time best-selling manual of essential know-how. For every angling specialty from pan-fishing in your neighborhood pond to big-game fishing in the deep sea, this book describes and illustrates all the key components—rods, reels, lines, hooks, knots, rigs, leaders, lures, live baits, dead baits and important accessories. No other book, regardless of size, contains so much useful, easily understood information on every level of freshwater and saltwater fishing—guaranteed!

Write today for information about *Complete Book of Baits, Rigs and Tackle* and other fine products from Wickstrom Publishers, Inc., which provides a variety of books, fishing charts and *Florida Sportsman* magazine.

WICKSTROM
PUBLISHERS, INCORPORATED
5901 S.W. 74 STREET, MIAMI, FLORIDA 33143

Books by Janna McMahan

CALLING HOME

THE OCEAN INSIDE

Published by Kensington Publishing Corporation